Happy Vale[n]
Day
1982
Love
Robin
Lisa

THE
COLORFUL
DU PONT
COMPANY

OTHER BOOKS BY P. J. WINGATE

Bandages of Soft Illusion
H. L. Mencken's Un-neglected Anniversary

CONTENTS

FOREWORD

P.J. Wingate does two things in this book. Probably both are intentional. One surely is. It is not certain about the other, but Phil is a clever writer, practiced at slipping thoughtful lessons into what seems to be simple narrative and down-home reminiscence. I have to assume he had both missions in mind.

His first task is to chronicle the dyes manufacturing business through the six decades in which it flourished in the American chemical industry generally, and in the Du Pont Company more particularly—to get it on paper before the colors fade. This he does in a rare fashion, as no outsider could. He catches the flavor and cadence of work inside a high-technology company, letting us into the world of *Bismarck Brown, Victoria Blue, Chicago Acid* (not what it would be in today's labeling system), and *Crystal Violet*. It all comes to life because Phil devotes as much attention to the personalities involved—mercurial, bizarre, stubborn and sometimes as brilliant as the colors they were trying to create out of organic chemical stews—as he gives to the chemistry and engineering involved, the more usual stuff of technological and business history. Phil assumes, and I think he is right on this, that what needs to be understood about technology in our society is its people and how they work, more than what they produce.

Phil Wingate is an inveterate people-watcher, charac-
ter collector, and sponge for anecdote. Some of his gleanings
we share in these pages. Had he done nothing more in this
book, I would be grateful to him for laying to rest the belief
that corporations, especially big ones, are peopled by sterile-
minded engineers and numbers-oriented managers. Wingate
learned long ago a secret that has been well kept from the
world outside the corporation; namely, that the people "in
there" are a fascinating, varied, and very human bunch, and
that a surprising number of them are having fun.

He does not quite level with you on one point though,
and the record should be set straight to reinforce his creden-
tials. In modesty, he concedes he has had a box seat on some
of the events of which he writes. In truth, he was in the middle of the action, and he works from first-hand information.
The author served for years in the dyes laboratory and production areas, and progressed to one of the senior executive
positions of Du Pont, a vice presidency with responsibility for
dozens of products, thousands of employees, and millions of
research dollars.

I must attend to the second accomplishment of the
book. It provides a rare insight into the innovation process.
Innovation is the subject of the hour, a national concern, a
buzz word, a topic of Congressional hearings and learned
monographs. We all regard innovation as important, and are
concerned that, in the United States, we may no longer have
enough of it, though we once seemed to excel at it.

Wingate scarcely uses the word, yet this whole chronicle is a shining set of case histories about the way the innovation process works. As no abstract treatise could, it shows
what it takes to create, develop, and make widely available
a new capsule of technology that has significant utility to the
public. Scientific principle or a basic discovery usually is important to it, sometimes essential, but in the innovation process, these may be only a start. You may have the chemical
formula for a new dye (often, as Phil reveals, the formula
was nowhere in sight and the research team was groping in

the dark, but putting up a bright front—another industrial secret let out of the bag) but that does not for a moment mean that the public will soon see a new product, or the manufacturer a dollar of profit. Innovation becomes consequential only through a progression of developmental and engineering accomplishments, marketing trials, and production scale-ups that take an idea from test tube, to pilot units, to full-scale commercial manufacture.

In this process there are all sorts of false starts, blind alleys, and mid-course corrections. Always, it seems, there are two overlying certainties: As the process moves forward it costs increasing amounts of money, which makes management nervous; and there is always someone in a position of authority who thinks the whole project is a terrible mistake. The worst of it is that sometimes that person is right.

Nonetheless, surprisingly, the innovation process does work a fair percentage of the time. The dye comes out in the intended color, it is waterproof, and it is just what Seventh Avenue wanted for its Spring line of fashions. Phil Wingate helps us understand how and why that is so. As he suggests, it is mostly because of people who have more than ordinary amounts of determination, skill, and nerve.

The chemistry in these pages may bother the uninitiated. As one of the unfortunates unwashed by formal education in science, I had trouble staying with the author here and there. I struggled with the "Monastral" blues and fell off the wagon when we rounded the Crystal Violet corner. This is a familiar problem for me, though, for as a lawyer in the executive's chair in Du Pont, I learned to live with presentations like Wingate's every day. My counsel to non-technical fellow sufferers is to stumble along behind the author as best you can. He takes you through the thickets with as much grace and patience as we can expect, and he probably is teaching you more than you realize.

His basic lessons will be lost on no one, scientist, engineer, or layman. He lets you see here that technologies and the products they spawn have an organic quality: They live and flourish in a particular time and setting. They do not go on forever, and even if they pass from the scene they cannot be set aside as failures. If they represent good technical work and useful contributions to society, they lead to other accomplishments. In this instance, the technology of dye making became an entering wedge to a half-century of progress in organic chemistry, marked by the creation of a vast array of man-made fibers, plastics, coatings, and other products in all but universal use today around the world.

Not only has Wingate got his hands on a story worth the telling; the residuals, as he calls them, lead you to believe that wherever there is good technology and innovation, the long-term benefits will far outstrip the imagination of the creators.

This book is dedicated to the thousands of men and women who ran the Du Pont Company's dye business for sixty-three years. They reached for rainbows and got their hands on a lot of them. Unfortunately, there were not enough pots of gold at the ends of these rainbows to keep the business profitable forever, so it died. However, during the digging operations a large number of other mines were uncovered and many of these are still highly productive.

AUTHOR'S REMARKS
THE ROLLER COASTER

The chemical industry, as it is known today in the United States, is an outgrowth of the manufacture of synthetic dyes. However, the United States has had a chemical industry of some sort ever since early colonial days. The colonists had whiskey, vinegar, and soap manufacturers who were practicing chemists even though they called themselves by other names such as distillers and soapers.

The whiskey makers were converting starches and sugars to alcohol and the vinegar producers were carrying the chemistry one step further by oxidizing the ethyl alcohol to acetic acid. These early fermenters and vinegar makers seldom produced their products on a large scale and mostly supplied themselves and the people in their immediate neighborhoods. The soapers also ran only small operations, extracting sodium and potassium hydroxide from ashes and using these alkaline liquors to react with animal fats to produce soaps.

The colonies also carried out some smelting operations to produce such things as iron, copper, and silver—all chemical processing operations. The use of mercury to extract silver from its ore was an old art in America long before Jamestown and Plymouth were settled. The Spanish brought the mercury process to Mexico and Peru nearly a hundred years before Capt. John Smith sailed up Chesapeake Bay, but this process was never used to any extent in the English-speaking part of North America until the great silver mines out west were discovered shortly before the Civil War.

The manufacture of gunpowder was also a fairly widespread chemical operation in colonial days although, again, the gunpowder people never thought of themselves as chemists. In fact, their ignorance of chemistry was usually so profound that they were fully justified in thinking of themselves as something else. This ignorance of the chemistry involved in what they were doing sometimes cost them their lives but more often it simply resulted in a product that behaved with exasperating inconsistency. It exploded when it was not supposed to and misfired so often that soldiers used their rifles as clubs almost as often as they fired them, thus an Indian armed only with a tomahawk was not at such a disadvantage as one might assume.

One of the great contributions, often overlooked by historians, that the French made to the Americans at the siege of Yorktown was to provide George Washington with reliable gunpowder. The French gunpowder was not as crucial to success at Yorktown as was the French Fleet under Count de Grasse, because without the fleet Lord Cornwallis would surely have escaped from the trap he was in, but it probably was more important than the French army under Count Rochembeau which aided Washington on land.

The French had gunpowder that was probably even better than that which the British had because France in those days had some of the best chemists in the world. One of these French chemists was Antoine Lavoisier who had made the study of gunpowder a major part of his life. All the world knew, even then, that gunpowder was a mixture of about 15 parts of charcoal with 10 parts of sulfur and 75 parts of potassium nitrate, or saltpeter as it is still called in the fireworks industry, but few people knew how to test the purity of these ingredients or how to correct deficiencies when they found them. They knew even less about the complex surface chemistry problems involved in getting the three ingredients intimately mixed. It would be nearly half a century later before American gunpowder manufacturers equalled the quality of the explosives which the French brought over with them for the crucial siege at Yorktown.

The compounding and fabrication of rubber materials also became a significant chemical industry after Goodyear learned how to vulcanize natural rubber latex a few years before the Civil War, but once again, as in the cases of the distillers, soapers, and gunpowder manufacturers, the rubber fabricators did not think of themselves as chemists. They were rubber makers.

Even after Americans began to manufacture such things as nitric and sulfuric acids, soda ash, and phosphate fertilizers, chemistry was thought of, if at all, as a European science and industry. In fact, Americans seldom thought about chemistry at all until World War I came along and the country was no longer able to obtain organic chemicals from Europe in general, and Germany in particular. The French, English, Swiss, and Italians were minor suppliers of chemicals but the Germans had almost a world monopoly in the field, despite the fact that Sir William Perkin, an Englishman, had made the first synthetic dye, mauve, and this discovery had really started the organic chemicals industry.

The Germans took the discovery by Perkin and ran with it so fast that by 1910 the term "German dye" was looked upon as one word just as "damn Yankee" became one word in the South after the Civil War.

Organic chemicals for medicine were also almost a German monopoly, and when the British blockade cut off the foreign markets that the Germans had been supplying, it hurt more than just appearances. The United States became almost desperate for both dyes and medicinal chemicals.

It was then that the Du Pont Company, which had been manufacturing gunpowder for a little over a century, starting with know-how that Eleuthère Irénée du Pont had obtained from the great Lavoisier himself, decided that it either had or could obtain enough chemical knowledge to permit it to manufacture some of the complex organic chemicals which the Germans had been supplying to the world.

This decision by the Du Pont Company to become more than just a gunpowder manufacturer was of enormous significance. It led to the development of the American chemical industry as it is known today, and during a period of half a century shifted the center of that chemical industry from the Rhine River in Germany to the Delaware River in America.

During the period from 1917 to 1965 chemistry, as it is now understood by the general public, grew rapidly in volume and diversity, with most of the growth occurring in that part of it which became known as organic chemistry.

Words have a habit of changing meaning as the years go by and this term "organic chemistry" now has to be explained. An organic farmer today is one who uses only chemicals found in nature while growing his crops, and organic food is food that is grown without the use of synthetic chemicals—only natural products. But organic chemistry, as the term originated and as it is still understood by chemists has just the opposite meaning. Organic chemistry almost always refers to synthetic chemicals and an organic chemist is not one who uses only natural products. The organic chemist makes synthetic chemicals which contain carbon. It is true that a couple of centuries ago even chemists thought organic chemicals could not be made synthetically; organic chemicals, they believed, were produced only by living plants and animals and could not be manufactured in the laboratory. And when a chemist named Friedrich Wohler made urea in the laboratory from inorganic starting materials he was the sensation of his day. Before Wohler urea came only from urine. Now it can be made in test tubes. Such is progress.

In any event, during the half century from 1920 to 1970, organic chemistry became a large industry in the United States and Wilmington, Delaware became recognized throughout the world as the center of that industry. Wilmington also became recognized as a world center for the science of chemistry. Chemistry, as a science, was widely diffused among the great universities of the nation but Wilmington was a major center because the Du Pont Company during that period had more Ph.D. chemists doing research work in chemistry than the universities of Harvard, Princeton, Stanford, and Duke combined.

During the period from 1875 to 1925 it had been necessary for an American chemist to spend at least a year or two at one of the great European universities, chiefly those in Germany or Switzerland, before he was accepted as a "complete" chemist, but in the half century that followed 1925 all this was reversed. European chemists felt compelled to spend a year or two in the United States before their peers around the world would accept them as masters in their field.

Furthermore, during the period from 1945 to 1965 chemistry became a glamour science, and popular writers referred to it as a magic genie which would work wonders and fill the needs of the human race in ways undreamed of a century or so before "Better things for better living through chemistry" became a nationally known Du Pont slogan.

There were many reasons why chemistry took on this aura of magic but the things that caught the public's attention most forcefully were those in the fields of health, food, and clothing.

The fabulous sulfa drugs were organic chemicals found to be "magic bullets" that entered the human body to kill the germs of such dread diseases as pneumonia and meningitis without killing the patient, and chemists were hotly pursuing research leads which promised to find more magic bullets. An array of vitamins had been defined chemically and food producers were using them to fortify their products so widely that vitamin deficiency diseases were projected to become a thing of the past. In fact, some enthusiasts declared that proper food, made nutritious and complete through the magic of chemistry, would not only produce intellectual competence in all people but might make it possible to grow geniuses on demand. Simply feed them the human equivalent of the honey bee's royal jelly used to grow queen bees. Not all people took such talk seriously but it did have its effect on the public attitude toward chemistry.

But no one questioned the fact that food for the human race had indeed become far more abundant because of a multitude of new chemical insecticides, fungicides, herbicides, and chemically balanced fertilizers that were making agricultural lands many times as productive, per acre, as they had been only a few decades ago. The specter of human starvation, which Malthus had gloomily predicted for the entire human race, had been pushed aside and existed only in those sections of the world where chemistry was not being utilized to work its wonders.

All of these boons to mankind had by no means come solely from along the banks of the Delaware, but many of them had, and the names that caught and held public attention most firmly—names such as neoprene, nylon, "Dacron," "Freon," and "Teflon"—were all from the Du Pont Company. Du Pont clearly was the most glamorous name in this glamorous field of chemistry. The first two of the five names given have become so universally used that they have become generic terms, but the world knew that nylon and neoprene— the wonder fiber and the wonder rubber—had both been invented by Du Pont.

All this must have been vastly irritating to Dow, Union Carbide, Allied Chemical, Hercules, Inc. and the many other companies that comprised the American chemical industry during this period of great glamour. However, to some extent, they all basked in the bright light being reflected from the Du Pont Company.

Then somewhere along about 1960 or 1965 things began to change and they changed with amazing speed. By 1975 chemistry had ceased to be a magic genie in the eyes of the general public, and became something close to Frankenstein's monster.

Chemicals were no longer thought of as magic bullets

which would cure the ills of the world but as poisons which were about to kill all forms of life on earth. The term "toxic chemical" became almost one word much like "German dye" had been before World War I and "damn Yankee" had been after the Civil War. Not only did the public come to think of chemicals as toxic; even worse, they were carcinogenic. If they didn't produce sudden death by poisoning they caused slow death from cancer. In addition, chemists were widely perceived as evil geniuses and chemical companies were thought of as amoral organizations which would happily poison the world for just a few extra dollars in profits.

During this period while chemistry was riding on this roller coaster of public opinion, from the height of esteem to the depth of distrust, I had a ringside seat inside the Du Pont Company and saw it all happen, first with pleasure mixed with amusement; later with dismay.

It was pleasant, during the 1940s and 1950s to be part of an industry which was so highly regarded but it was also somewhat amusing to think about the vast difference that existed between the way the public perceived chemists and the way they really were.

When chemists reported their discoveries, either orally or in written documents, they almost invariably managed to give the impression that what they had accomplished was the product of carefully planned research, conceived in pure logic and nursed to glorious maturity with regular feedings of enriched ratiocination. In short, chemists were geniuses who moved surely and swiftly along the road to progress until they came upon the pot of gold which logic and a blinding flash of wisdom, much like what struck St. Paul on the road to Damascus, told them was sure to be there.

Actually what they did, in most cases, was to grope their way along the road, often on hands and knees, not quite sure what they were seeking, until they stumbled upon something that looked as if it might be useful. Then they went back, redefined their goals and jubilantly declared to their associates and bosses, as well as to the rest of the world: "Here is what I was looking for!" Often the product they came up with was something not even faintly related to what they had set out to find. In fact, some of their most spectacular success stories were of just this sort.

This explanation of how most chemists work should not be looked upon as an attempt to belittle them because it did require genius of a sort to recognize the nuggets of gold in the sorry-looking messes which usually came out of their test tubes. But it was genius of a different kind from the pure logic which the chemists and their publicists proclaimed so loudly. The products which came out of most early experiments tend to look as useless as hunks of road tar when they are viewed by ordinary mortals but those skilled in the art and science of chemistry can sometimes look at these amorphous chunks of goop and see in them a new textile fiber or a magic bullet to cure leprosy.

If the word genius can properly be applied to any member of the human race then there probably are some chemists who fit the term; but, if so, their genius lies in the keenness of their observations, the intensity of their searching, and in their ability to look at apparently unrelated facts found in their laboratories and journals to see how they all fit together.

Just why chemistry was given a roller coaster ride from the peak of favor to the pit of disfavor has always been something of a mystery. It may be partly because the public slowly began to believe that chemistry has some hazards that chemists themselves had never dreamed of. If so, there is some justification for the change in public attitude because as research continues, a few hidden hazards are uncovered every year. Just as physicists, at first, never dreamed that their harmless looking X-rays could do damage as well as good, so did chemists fail, at first, to understand that even such a common and useful chemical as benzene must be handled carefully to avoid excess exposure to it. It also may be partly because the public began to look upon chemists as one-dimensional people interested in nothing except the contents of their test tubes. This is a false perception as can be seen by looking at the thoroughly three-dimensional people who operated the Du Pont Company's dye business for 63 years.

PERKIN'S MARVELOUS MAUVE

1

nce a year about five hundred chemists and their spouses assemble at the Plaza Hotel, just off New York's Central Park, to eat, drink, and pay tribute to the winner of the Perkin medal, awarded annually by the American Section of the Society of Chemical Industry to a distinguished chemist.

It is a fashionable affair, which fits well with the quiet elegance of the Plaza and many members of the nobility and gentry of industrial chemistry are present each year. The women wear formal gowns and the men in their tuxedos and long-tailed coats look much like penguins except for just one thing. The black and white effect is broken by the mauve colored ties which the men all wear.

That is to say, the men wear ties that are a rather muddy, washed-out shade of pink or purple. Mauve has not been a popular color since the "mauve decade" of the 1870s, but mauve ties have long been required at Perkin dinners because this somewhat drab color was invented by Sir William Henry Perkin in 1856 and was the first synthetic dye ever made.

Before Sir William made his great discovery the world was a comparatively dull place because all dyes for clothing had to be extracted from some living plant or animal source and there was never enough colored material available to meet the demand. Color was prized more highly then because it was so scarce.

In 1981 the Perkin dinner was presided over by Dr. Edward G. Jefferson, President of the American Section of the Society of Chemical Industry, and President and Chairman-elect of the Du Pont Company. After the cocktail hour, when the guests were all seated at their assigned tables, Dr. Jefferson welcomed them and congratulated the gentlemen because they all were wearing their mauve ties.

"More of these ties are now available," he said, "since a new batch of mauve dye has been approved by the Society. As some of you know, the Du Pont Company was asked to produce a new lot of mauve two years ago and we confidently assigned this task to our dye experts at the Chambers Works. Unfortunately, our first attempt to produce this gorgeous hue failed so badly that the material was flatly rejected by the Society's standards committee and we had to try again. Again we failed, but on the third attempt we were successful although I'm told that even then our product barely got by.

"In any event, we were so chastened by the experience that the Du Pont Company decided to go out of the manufacture of dyes, and we have just recently sold our entire dye business."

This humble confession produced a roar of laughter and probably saved Dr. Jefferson from a few darts which might otherwise have been thrown at him during the course of the evening, since Du Pont's departure from the dye business was still exciting some comments in the chemical industry. The Chairman's remarks were perhaps as graceful a farewell as could have been devised in closing a venture which had absorbed Du Pont for over sixty years and had not only given the Company a colorful half-century but had led directly or indirectly to products that now produce annual sales of over ten billion dollars.

So Perkin's discovery of mauve, which started it all, was a significant development for the organic chemicals industry and, as will be seen, it was typical of much of the progress that has occurred in this field during the past half-century.

William Perkin was born in London in 1838, only ten years after Wohler first showed that urea could be made from inorganic materials and did not have to be derived from the urine of animals. Before Wohler's discovery it had been assumed that all organic chemicals must come from living things—plants or animals. Organic chemistry was not even a subject for study in the universities of the world in those days. Nevertheless, there was a strong demand for organic chemicals.

One product much in demand by all who traveled to tropical countries, as many Englishmen did, was quinine. It was extracted from the bark of cinchona trees and was steadily in short supply.

In 1856 when Perkin was only 18 years old and a student in the Royal College of Chemistry in London, he decided to do something about the chronic shortage of quinine, which offered the only known treatment for malaria.

Perkin knew that quinine contained nitrogen, hydrogen, and carbon; but that was just about all he knew concerning the chemical composition of this complex compound. But he also knew that aniline, of which he had a small supply, contained only nitrogen, hydrogen, and carbon. So, armed with this vast supply of ignorance and the optimism which characterizes youth, he decided to make quinine by oxidizing aniline with potassium dichromate.

From such strange mixtures, plus a generous supply of luck, have come many of the great discoveries of organic chemistry during the past century and a half. Luck was with Perkin because the aniline, unknown to him, contained substantial amounts of toluidines, both ortho and para, materials which look much like aniline. So when he oxidized his aniline he produced, along with a lot of tarry material, small amounts of several dyes—chiefly safranine and fuchsine dyes; red, pink, and purple materials never seen before, and even in this case well hidden in the tars.

There was, of course, not a single molecule of quinine in Perkin's tarry mass and nearly a century would elapse before anyone learned how to make quinine in the laboratory. Then Robert Woodward did the trick in his laboratory at Harvard and received a Nobel prize for his efforts in synthesis. However, quinine for medicine is still extracted from trees because that is a cheaper route than Woodward's laboratory synthesis. So it was no easy assignment that Perkin gave himself, and if he had known many times as much chemistry as he did, he almost certainly would not have tried to make quinine by oxidizing aniline.

But having made a hunk of what looked like road tar, instead of quinine, Perkin then showed a true flash of genius. He did not throw his sticky mess into the trash can, as most people would have done, but decided to extract from it the clear crystals of quinine that he hoped were hiding within it. There were no quinine molecules present; but, in trying to purify this tarry product he noticed that in certain lights it had a purplish sheen about it, and when a drop diluted with water fell on his shirt front, he saw a purplish pink color spread out from the black drop at the center—Mauve!

There was still a vast amount of trial and error work before Perkin was able to isolate enough dye to color even one necktie but he kept at it and was shrewd enough to realize that he had stumbled on to something important. He patented his discovery in 1856 and in 1857 built, near Harrow in England, the first synthetic dye plant the world had ever seen.

If the Du Pont Company's dye experts at Chambers Works really had as much trouble making mauve as Dr. Jefferson claimed, it was still small compared to the problems Perkin encountered in that first plant. His raw materials varied in composition and it was a long time before he learned that the toluidine impurities were so crucial. Also the temperature reached when the aniline and dichromate were mixed was crucial, and Perkin was unable to control this temperature well because he had inadequate cooling and agitation in his reactor. Perkin's first mauve in the laboratory was a grand mixture of red, pink, and purple dyes and so were all the lots that he made in his plant, with no two exactly alike. In fact, it is almost certain that no two lots of mauve ever made were exactly alike, or even very close to being alike if they were analyzed by sophisticated chemical techniques. Mauve was always a real dog's breakfast with a dozen or two individual dyes in it along with scores of other impurities helping to give it that somewhat muddy look it always has. About all Perkin could hope for was that each lot of mauve would be some hue of pinkish-purple or purplish-pink. And that is just about all any manufacturer today can expect.

The late Tallulah Bankhead, who starred on stage and screen, made no attempt to hide the fact that she liked the bohemian life. "I am," she once told a reporter, "as pure as the driven slush." Not being able to research this remark, it probably can be said that Miss Bankhead was at least as pure as Perkin's mauve. It is a scientific fact about the dye business that the closer a dye comes to being one chemical entity the brighter and purer its hue becomes, and the more impurities it contains the muddier it looks.

There is a sound principle of physics behind this observation because any colored compound absorbs certain wave lengths of light and reflects others. If it absorbs all wave lengths of light except red, and reflects red, then the eye sees it as a red dye. If it reflects only blue wave lengths then it is a blue dye, but if it is a grand mixture and reflects many hues, and also absorbs many, then it is not a bright, clearly defined dye. It may look a lot like mauve.

While all this is true, it probably gives a misleading impression of Perkin's mauve, which really was the marvel of its time. In the kingdom of the blind a one-eyed man is likely to be made a monarch, and so it was with mauve.

Perkin sold mauve as fast as he could produce it, and all wealthy people in Europe and America wanted to have something mauve-colored. The "mauve decade" really lasted twenty years—from the early 1860s to 1880, by which time the German and English manufacturers of synthetic dyes had a large roster of more attractive products. Not only were they much cleaner and brighter in tone but many of them did not fade as badly, when exposed to light and washing, as mauve did.

But Perkin started it all and he did not stop with mauve despite its enormous early popularity. He learned how to synthesize the ancient red dye which had always in the past been extracted from the madder plant. This was alizarin, a red dye that had been popular as a military uniform dye for centuries. However, it would be a mistake to assume that all the red coats that the British wore when opposing George Washington were dyed with alizarin. The Royal Army in those days made do with whatever was available so the hues of the Red Coats probably varied as least as much as the different lots of Perkin's mauve.

Perkin's plants producing mauve, alizarin, and the many other dyes which his research soon developed were a huge and instant success story. He gave the British Empire a head start in what was soon to become a very large industry even though the Germans later ran away with the dye markets of the world when Perkin began to devote most of his time and attention to research in other fields.

There he was equally successful and proved that he was a scientist of the first rank. He discovered what the textbooks of chemistry still call "the Perkin reaction," which is a process for making unsaturated acids by reacting aromatic aldehydes with the salts of fatty acids. Cinnamic acid and coumarin, two materials important as taste and odor additives, were two of his specific discoveries. He also became an authority on color theory and made a great contribution to the understanding of the relationship between chemical composition and the rotation of the plane of polarized light.

Perkin received a host of scientific honors in England and abroad and received the Royal medal of the Royal Society in 1879 and the Davy medal in 1889. The Davy medal was in honor of Sir Humphrey Davy, the chemist who first isolated sodium and potassium.

Queen Victoria ignored him as a candidate for knighthood throughout her long reign, despite his industrial and scientific accomplishments. The record does not show why the Queen behaved this way and chemists have long been puzzled by her failure to honor him, since she knighted many lesser scientists and industrialists.

Perhaps Victoria was offended by what she probably regarded as the loose morals of the "mauve decade" and thought that the somewhat lurid shade of mauve had contributed to this laxity. So perhaps she simply resolved to give no encouragement to mauve or its inventor. Her son, Edward VII, had no such scruples and knighted Perkin in 1906, a few years after Victoria had died and he ascended to the throne. The Queen was undeniably victorian but Edward was not, even though he lived through much of the same period of time.

In addition to being moralistic, Victoria may also have been ungrateful, because Perkin and his associates in the dye business made a habit of naming any new particularly brilliant dye which they developed in her honor.

There were, for example, the following new dyes, all much cleaner in appearance than mauve, named in her honor:

> *Victoria Blue B*
> *Victoria Blue R*
> *Victoria Pure Blue BO*

Dye chemists have long had a practice of putting letters after the name of a dye to indicate some special hue or other property of a color. For example, *Victoria Blue B* simply meant a blue shade of blue while *Victoria Blue R* meant a red shade of blue.

The last of the three dyes listed above was by far the clearest and brightest of the group, hence the word *Pure,* while the letters, *BO,* meant that it was *brighter* than an *older* dye already being sold. All this happened long before

Lifebuoy soap invented the term *BO* meaning *body odor,* so there is no reason to think that the Queen was offended by the name of *Victoria Pure Blue BO* or took it as a slur against her personal daintiness. There is no reason to believe that Victoria smelled any less sweet than any other monarch of her time.

Also, there is no reason to think that Queen Victoria simply did not like chemists, because she cast a decisive vote in favor of the Scotch chemist, James Simpson, who got involved with two Americans, Dr. Long of Georgia and Dr. Morton of Boston in an argument about the relative merits of chloroform and ether as an anesthetic. This argument lasted for four or five decades with Simpson supporting chloroform and the Americans favoring ether. Queen Victoria settled the argument in England by deciding to use chloroform during the birth of her seventh child. If chloroform was good enough for the Queen it was good enough for any Briton, and chloroform became the anesthetic of choice in most of the English-speaking world for half a century—until doctors found strong evidence that it injures the liver.

Today chloroform is on the list of suspected carcinogens and every now and then a reporter creates a sensation by declaring traces of it to be present in the drinking water of some city. These stories ignore the fact that from 1870 to 1920 over twenty-five million people were exposed to massive doses of chloroform during surgery without causing an epidemic of cancer.

It is an interesting fact that after ether became the preferred anesthetic in about 1920, it was finally replaced in the 1950s by Fluothane, a chemical cousin of chloroform developed by Dr. Charles Suckling of the Imperial Chemical Industries, the firm which eventually took over Perkin's dye plants. Fluothane is more stable than chloroform and does not damage the liver. The increased stability of Fluothane apparently comes from the replacement of chlorine atoms by fluorine and bromine in a molecule otherwise much like chloroform.

In any event, when Sir William Henry Perkin died in 1907 he was loaded with all sorts of honors including a knighthood, and his place in history is secure.

Even mauve itself, though it ceased to be a dye of importance about a hundred years ago, will continue to be thought of whenever the industrial chemists assemble to honor one of their members with the Perkin medal. Some of those present may think first about the Plaza bar and its salty oysters on the half shell, and some may think of tea and a pastry in the Plaza's tearoom on the main floor. Some may think of the expensive jewelry on display in shops around the lobby and a few may even imagine that they can hear faint echos from the heels of Kay Thompson's fabulous, fictional little girl, Eloise, as she races along the corridors of the Plaza. Others may think the speeches introducing the guest of honor tend to be too long, and still others may think the medalist is sometimes inclined to devote too much time to his own glorification, and nearly all of them may think that the reception, after the medal has been awarded, is a waste of food and drink on guests who are already filled to capacity.

But all of them will look at those ties in their washed out shades of pink, red, and purple and think of Perkin and his marvelous mauve.

FROM AZO BLACK AND BISMARCK BROWN TO XYLENE YELLOW AND ZAPON RED

2

efore Perkin made his great discovery in 1856 even kings had trouble finding enough dye to color their royal raiment. A monarch in those days, unless he was a truly mighty one, usually had the collar of his royal robe dyed with cochineal crimson or tyrian purple but the rest of his cloak was likely to be a faded indigo blue, a streaky alizarin red, or some muddy-looking mixture of these two dyes obtained from plant sources. In fact, the king's coat, except for its collar, might be an undyed dirty white.

It was just too costly to obtain enough cochineal insects for the crimson or enough shellfish (murex brandaris) for the purple, to color an entire robe. Even indigo and madder plants were too scarce to permit dukes, counts, and similar noble pretenders to dye their coats blue or red, so these worthy fellows often wore butternut brown or dirty white, like the lesser kings did. However, the rug makers of Persia, Turkey, and India had managed somehow, for centuries, to find the dye needed to color their products.

Even after Perkin began to manufacture commercial quantities of mauve in 1857 in his plant outside London, the shortage of dyes continued for a decade or so. But the age of synthetic dyes had finally arrived and during the quarter of a century that followed 1860, more than 200 chemically different dyes, in every hue of the rainbow, were offered to the clothing industry in commercial quantities, and over 5000 colored substances were investigated in the chemical laboratories of Europe. It was like an explosion in a paint factory.

Although Perkin's mauve in England was the spark which set off the explosion, the explosion itself occurred mostly in Germany. The German chemists went on a color-making binge which lasted half a century. While most of their new colored materials were never offered to the public as dyes, for one reason or another, and many of the several hundred which were offered never became important commercially, the manufacture of dyes did become a large industry during the period from 1870 to 1900.

Some historians have expressed surprise that England, which started the synthetic dye business, allowed Germany to run away with most of the prizes in this industry which paid off so handsomely for many decades. However, the dominant position quickly established by Germany was never surprising to chemists of that period because they knew that the synthetic dyes were derived from benzene and other coal tar chemicals, a field in which German chemists had established themselves as masters even before 1850.

The list of German chemical masters is a long one but two names stand out in the early history of dyes and organic chemistry: Kekule and Beilstein.

German chemists had known for several decades that a host of organic chemicals could be distilled from coal and they knew that many of these chemicals, such as aniline and phenol, were derived from a basic molecule, benzene, also found in coal.

This basic molecule, benzene, had troubled chemists ever since they began to experiment with it, because it behaved in ways that could not be explained using the theories that had worked so well for other compounds containing only carbon and hydrogen. This puzzlement about benzene, this inability to explain why it behaved the way it did, went on for decades and many distinguished chemists tried to write a formula for it which would be free of internal contradictions. Some of the famous chemists who took a crack at the problem were Armstrong, Ladenburg, Thiele, and Thompson, and their formulas all had some merits. But they also had serious defects.

Then Friedrick August Kekule, whose life span, 1829–1896, put him squarely in the middle of the dye explosion, came up with one of the most useful and enduring concepts in the history of organic chemistry—the "benzene ring." There are many apocryphal stories about how the benzene ring was conceived, and one of them says that Kekule drank too much beer one day while he was struggling with the benzene problem, and in his dreams that night saw snakes swimming in the air above his bed with each snake trying to swallow its own tail.

In any event, the benzene ring which Kekule finally presented to the scientific world was a closed figure, a hexagon, with each of its six angles representing the six carbon atoms known to be in a benzene molecule. Kekule's benzene ring has withstood the attacks of all critics for over a century. Even modern organic chemists, steeped in clouds of electrons and devoted to sophisticated analytical devices such as nuclear magnetic resonators, still find it to be a flawless concept.

Kekule was for many years professor of chemistry at the University of Ghent and the University of Bonn, but he was temporarily working with Stenhouse in London when Perkin discovered mauve in 1856. Kekule may have learned of this sensational development from young Perkin himself but more probably he learned of it from Perkin's teacher, August Wilhelm Von Hoffman, another German temporarily in England, and also an expert on coal tar chemistry. It is likely that by 1860 young Perkin's discovery was more widely known in Germany than it was in England.

And Germany was prepared to run with the new information partly because of the work being done by the second of the two famous names given above: Beilstein.

Friedrick Konrad Beilstein was the son of German parents but was born in St. Petersburg, Russia. He studied chemistry at Heidelberg, Munich, and Göttingen and became professor of chemistry at the Imperial Technological Institute in St. Petersburg, where he succeeded Mendelyeev, the man who had shown that the elements making up all matter were not just a jumble but could be arranged in a table which made sense and permitted useful predictions to be made.

Perhaps Beilstein was influenced by his predecessor, Mendeleev, but in any event Beilstein made it his life's work to bring some organization to the jumble of organic chemistry that had reached a monumental size during the half century following Wohler's demonstration in 1828, that organic chemicals did not have to originate in living plants or animals. Thousands of these carbon containing molecules had been made in the laboratory and the Germans had shown that many thousands of new compounds could be made from such building blocks as benzene, aniline, phenol, and naphthalene, which could be driven from coal by heating it. But this welter of information existed chiefly as a vast jumble that swamped most people when they tried to evaluate it or use it as a basis for further researches.

Then Beilstein showed that the jumble could be organized, classified, and categorized so as to bring some sense to it. He did this in one of the most remarkable books ever written: *Beilstein's Handbuch der Organischen Chemie.*

The first edition of Beilstein's handbook appeared in 1881–82, in two volumes, consisting of 2200 pages, which described 15,000 compounds of carbon. But, because he had been organizing the material in it for over a decade, it had been available to the dye experts of Germany in published or unpublished form throughout the dye explosion.

Chemists found Beilstein's handbook so useful that he followed the first edition with a second in 1885–89 and expanded it to three volumes of 4080 pages. This process of expansion and revision continued through Beilstein's life and became an industry conducted by the Beilstein Institute of

Frankfurt, Germany, which always has a ready market for its product. A new model is always in some stage of preparation and the raw material from which it is assembled has never ceased to expand. The most recent series consisted of 27 volumes. The Beilstein Institute claims that the Beilstein "handbook," a term which amuses all students who first look at it in all its glory of 27 large volumes, "is unique among handbooks of organic chemistry in that it provides a collection of critically examined and exactly reproduced data on the known carbon compounds. It is in this respect superior to all other straight bibliographical documentation and series of abstracts."

No organic chemist disputes this boast by the Beilstein Institute, and every major chemical center in the world tries to have a copy of Beilstein on the shelves of its library. Professors of organic chemistry still generally advise their students to "look it up in Beilstein" before proceeding with a proposed research program. But Beilstein itself has become so large and complex that the publisher puts out a 35 page booklet called *How to Use Beilstein*, and professors usually spend a lecture or two explaining it to their students.

Beilstein categorizes its thousands of compounds in various ways but one classification breaks them down into acyclic, isocyclic, and heterocyclic categories. The isocyclic compounds have ring structures, like Kekule's "benzene ring," that contain only carbon, and the heterocyclic compounds contain one or more other elements, such as nitrogen or oxygen, along with carbon in the ring. These two categories seldom confuse beginning students but the acyclic category does. They frequently think that acyclic means some special kind of ring, instead of no ring at all. Their professors tell them about the New York policeman who was once assigned the job of keeping order in one block during a Communist parade on Fifth Avenue on May 1.

Some hecklers began to hoot at the paraders and even to throw things at them. Whereupon the cop collared one of the hecklers and told him sternly: "You damn Communists have got to behave yourselves on my block."

"You don't understand," the heckler replied, "I am an anti-Communist!"

"I don't give a damn what kind of a Communist you are," the cop replied. "You have to be orderly on my block."

But while Beilstein baffles beginners today and may have to some extent done the same in 1881, professionals have always found it to be enormously useful, and the dye chemists of those early days surely used it to help them get a leg up in the competition with England for the dye market.

Both the English and the Germans rather quickly determined that Perkin's mauve was a mixture of several safranine dyes (phenazines) and triphenyl methane dyes. Then the triphenyl methane dyes soon were developed into an entire series of dyes, all stemming from benzene (phenyl) or its first derivative, aniline. Aniline, in fact, became such an important building block for the new synthetic dyes that they were once all called "aniline dyes" until later developments produced so many important dyes not derived from aniline. Then they were called "coal tar" dyes for a while until further developments made that term obsolete also.

One derivative of aniline that was very important in the early history of synthetic dyes was dimethyl aniline, a compound with two methyl groups attached to the one nitrogen atom in aniline. The impurities in Perkin's aniline that caused him to obtain a dye were also methyl anilines but of a different sort; the methyl groups in Perkin's impurities were attached to the phenyl group itself and not to the nitrogen atom.

Anyway, both the Germans and the English found that if three dimethyl aniline molecules were tied together through a central carbon atom (the methane carbon) a powerful dye known as crystal violet was produced. This very early dye was, oddly enough, the most powerful dye, tinctorially, ever synthesized. That is to say, one ounce of crystal violet would color a greater volume of water than any other dye that has ever been made. It never was a good dye for coloring wool, cotton, or any other fiber even though it was used as a cloth dye in early days, but it was developed for other important uses, and over a million pounds of it continued to be made annually even a hundred years after it was first discovered.

The triphenyl methane dyes did much to give the Germans their early lead in dye manufacture because the habit of organization, which the Germans apparently had as an act of nature and which was surely encouraged by Beilstein and his associates, worked quickly to give them a mastery of the triphenyl methane dyes.

Having found that dimethyl aniline was a good building block for dyes, the Germans, with their Beilstein training helping them, quickly investigated the many other obvious candidates such as diethyl aniline, dipropyl aniline, dibutyl aniline and dozens of other similar compounds such as chloro dimethyl aniline and bromo dimethyl aniline. All of these materials made dyes somewhat similar to crystal violet and the Germans probably made several hundreds of them before concluding that, all things considered, the first one of them, crystal violet, was the best. The dye from diethyl aniline, called ethyl violet, did become a commercial product but it never reached the importance of crystal violet.

An important building block for the new dyes was discovered by Wilhelm Michler, another German whose relatively short career, 1846 to 1889, also placed him in the middle of the dye explosion. Michler found that he could gain better control of the dye-making process if he first tied just two dimethyl aniline molecules together by reacting dimethyl aniline with phosgene. The product became known as Michler's ketone.

The flow of basic information did not always go from England to Germany and in the case of Michler's ketone, it went in the opposite direction. The English dye chemists seized upon Michler's ketone and made a very valuable dye by reacting it with phenyl alpha naphthylamine. It was perhaps the cleanest looking blue dye ever seen up to that time and the English decided to name it in honor of Queen Victoria, so they called the new dye *Victoria Blue B*. The letter *B* at the end of the name simply indicated that the dye was a pure blue. However, they soon discovered that an even-brighter, cleaner looking blue could be made by reacting ethyl ketone with ethyl alpha naphthylamine. So they called this improved blue dye *Victoria Pure Blue BO*.

Queen Victoria probably was pleased by these flattering names but if so she did not respond by giving any special honors, such as a knighthood, to either the inventors or the manufacturers of *Victoria Blue B* and *Victoria Pure Blue BO*. Perhaps she thought they had already been properly rewarded when she permitted them to use her name and thereby promote the sale of their products. While the Victoria blues were better dyes than crystal violet, dyeing cloth more evenly and giving a more pleasing coloration to the cloth, they still were very poor dyes—poor in light fastness and fastness to washing, among other things. Nevertheless, during the last twenty years of Victoria's reign, most wealthy Britons managed to have some item of clothing—a tie, handkerchief, scarf, or blouse—which had the clean blue hue of *Victoria Pure Blue BO*.

Both the Germans and the English kept looking for a triaryl methane dye which would be superior to crystal violet and the Victoria blues and they made scores of them by the various processes they found would produce these triaryl methane dyes. The word "triaryl" replaced triphenyl when it became known that naphthalene and other ring structures could, sometimes with advantage, replace one or more of the phenyl groups in a triphenyl methane dye.

The simplest method of making a triaryl methane dye was to react the proper amine, for example dimethyl aniline with phosgene, then zinc chloride, and finally with phosphorous oxy chloride. Starting with dimethyl aniline, the dye produced was crystal violet, while starting with diethyl aniline led to the dye known as ethyl violet. If a mixture of dimethyl aniline and diethyl aniline was used then four different dyes were produced, all mixed together, but if three amines—say dimethyl aniline, diethyl aniline, and dipropyl aniline—were used to start with, then eight chemically different dyes were produced. In these cases the end products were always mixtures which, in general, were duller in shade than a single pure dye.

The Michler's ketone process permitted better control of the product and also permitted other amines, such as phenyl alpha naphthylamine and ethyl alpha naphthylamine to be easily incorporated into the dye molecule. Ethyl ketone served a similar purpose and was just like Michler's ketone except that it was made from diethyl aniline instead of dimethyl aniline.

Triaryl methane dyes were also made by both the English and German chemists by a process involving Michler's hydrol. This process gave dyes that were slightly different from those made by the other processes but the basic deficiencies of triaryl methane dyes—poor light fastness, poor wash fastness, and streaky dyeing—always remained the same, regardless of the manufacturing process.

While the British and Germans remained locked in combat centered about the triaryl methane dyes, and with the issue still in doubt, there then occurred the most important development in the entire history of synthetic coloring materials. Azo dyes burst upon the scene like a star-shell at a fourth of July fireworks display, scattering color in all directions.

The word azo is short for the French word for nitrogen—azote. So, an azo dye was one containing nitrogen but this definition was not really definitive because the triaryl methane dyes also contained nitrogen. Actually, it would have been more precisely descriptive if the azo dyes had been called diazo dyes, meaning two nitrogens, because all azo dyes do contain at least two nitrogen atoms linked in a structure which chemists write in the following manner:

$$-N:N-$$

The two dashes indicate that other organic groups, usually benzene or naphthalene derivatives, are attached to the two doubly bonded nitrogen atoms in the middle.

The azo dyes really had their beginning in 1858, only one year after Perkin built his first synthetic dye plant, when Peter Griess, an Englishman born in Germany, showed how to diazotize an amine group. That is, he showed how to add an additional nitrogen atom to a molecule that already has one nitrogen atom. But Griess did not understand the importance of what he had done and nothing further occurred for seven years. Then another German chemist named Martius showed that it was possible to make a brown dye by letting a diazotized amine react with another amine. Actually Martius caused diazotized metaphenylene diamine to react with fresh metaphenylene diamine to give the first real azo dye.

Martius was not at all sure what he really had done, and later work showed that he had, like Perkin before him, made a mixture of dyes—at least four or five different dye molecules. However, he saw that what he had was colored brown and that it could be used to dye cotton. He was so proud of his new product that he decided to call it *Bismarck Brown,* in honor of Otto von Bismarck, the chancellor of Germany who had already made a great name for himself in European political circles.

Bismarck Brown has been described as a bronze color, a yellow-orange color, and a brownish-yellow color. It probably was all of those things because, again just like mauve, it varied in shade from lot to lot, and the Berlin plant built by Martius to make it soon found it desirable to make two shades, a greenish shade called *Bismarck Brown G* and a reddish shade called *Bismarck Brown R.* Neither type was a great dye, as measured by modern standards, but both were far better, in most respects, than the triaryl methane dyes.

Brown became a very popular color in Germany and remains so to this day even though Hitler's brown-shirted Nazis did a lot to discredit it.

History does not reveal whether Bismarck was more pleased to have a color named in his honor than Queen Victoria was by the Victoria blues named for her. The old "Iron Chancellor" liked to maintain a pose of not being affected by either praise or criticism and it is possible that he was more pleased when they named a pickled herring in his honor and called it *Bismarck Herring.*

In any event, the azo dyes soon gave Germany a clear lead over England, for the first time, and that lead was extended steadily for the next half-century. Kekule, of benzene ring fame, helped the Germans in their azo dye development by explaining how to control the coupling of the diazo salts, discovered by Griess, with the other component which was needed to make an azo dye.

And although Kekule was not aware of all the things that would couple with a diazo salt, the final list turned out to be a long one. It included aromatic hydroxy compounds such as phenols and naphthols, aromatic amines, compounds with reactive methylene groups, and even some hydrocarbons. However, the most important of these coupling compounds turned out to be derivatives of naphthalene.

Naphthalene is a close cousin of benzene. Chemists struggled with its complex chemistry for years and never really understood it until after Kekule came out with his benzene ring theory. Then other chemists came to realize that naphthalene really consisted of two benzene rings joined together like Siamese twins, sharing the same backbone.

Then naphthalene began to make sense to chemists and when azo dyes came along they were ready to make coupling components derived from naphthalene. There were hundreds of these components and two dozen or so of these became commercially important. The full chemical names of these coupling components were often so long that chemists began to give them single letter names. For example "H acid" was really 1 amino, 6 hydroxy, 3–6 naphthalene disulfonic acid. And "J acid" was really 2 amino, 5 hydroxy naphthalene sulfonic acid. "A acid" was 3,5 dihydroxy, 2,7 naphthalene disulfonic acid and "S acid" was 8 amino, 1 hydroxynaphthalene, 5 sulfonic acid.

And so it went on and on for pages but the chemists, having adopted a simple system which would have pleased Beilstein in his passion for order, would not stick with a simple letter system. They felt compelled to name some of their naphthalene sulfonic acid coupling components after the inventor and so there was "Laurents Acid," "Tobias Acid," "Koch's Acid" and others.

Somehow even "Chicago Acid" sneaked into the list. There was no inventor named Chicago and history does not say how this coupling component got its name. Perhaps some reader of poetry grew weary of Carl Sandburg's labelling of Chicago as hog butcher to the world and thought the hometown of the Chicago Cubs needed some more dignified item to identify with. Anyway, "Chicago Acid" is 8 amino, 1 hydroxy, 5,7 naphthalene disulfonic acid.

With a long list of different diazo salts and an even longer list of coupling components to go with it the combinations of azo dyes was almost infinite, and the Germans went into a frenzy of new azo dyes which put their work on the triphenyl methane dyes to shame.

They not only made every hue in the rainbow but they made cotton dyes, wool dyes, acid dyes, dyes that were fixed on fiber by oxidizing them with chromate, premetallized dyes, dyes that were formed right on the fiber, and dozens of other types.

The English did not give up when azo dyes appeared on the scene and British chemists contributed importantly to many of these developments. Even the Swiss, French, and Italians got into the act but their contributions, while sometimes technically sophisticated, were not important commercially in the early days of synthetic dyes, and only the Swiss became a significant factor after 1900.

The fireworks in dyes did not end with the azo explosion. Other important developments continued to follow the azo dyes from time to time in the future. Among these new developments were sulfur colors and anthraquinone dyes. The sulfur color dyes made a moderate impact when they first appeared but they soon dwindled into insignificance. The anthraquinone dyes were vastly more important and have continued to be so even until today, but the relative importance of the azo dyes can be stated most briefly by noting that the total pounds of azo dyes sold in the past century exceeds the total of the next three largest categories. Nevertheless, it would be a mistake to belittle the importance of the anthraquinone dyes. They represent some of the highest quality dyes ever produced and the chemistry involved in making them is the most complex of all dye chemistry.

The many other categories of dyes, such as the dyes used in color photography, reflect even more sophisticated chemistry but never became important on a pound/volume basis or in dollars. A comprehensive review of all dyes would require several volumes the size of those in Beilstein's handbook and so will be avoided here.

All that is intended in this chapter is to give some indication of how complex and technical the manufacture of dyes had become by 1900. When the guns of August boomed out to announce the start of World War I, the chemists of Europe, mostly in Germany and England, had invested more than a thousand man-years in development of a technology which involved much science but also quite a bit of "art," a term scientists use to describe the science that they cannot really define.

THE WORLD OF DYES IN 1917

3

Mark Twain has been a popular author in Germany for a century or so and even today his books, in both English and German, can be found in most good bookstores there. His popularity with the Germans was due primarily, of course, to the humor in what he wrote, but the Germans also liked the fact that he made a determined effort to learn the language when he lived there for a while. He gave up the project long before it was completed, and concluded that no one, except a native, would ever be able to master "that awful German language."

Old Mark said that when a German started a sentence, he promptly dived under the surface of the thought being expressed, like an otter hunting for fish, and was not seen again for two or three lines or perhaps a paragraph until, at the end of the sentence, he came up again holding a verb in his mouth. The Germans must have recognized some truth in this because they do write very long sentences and usually end them with a verb. A German can start talking about a man and proceed to relate his ancestry, date of birth, occupation, political beliefs, religion, and a dozen other things about him, without giving any clue as to whether the man has just been elected to public office or shot—until that verb shows up at the end.

Consequently, Mark Twain was not alone in having

trouble with German; most English speaking people do. So it is not surprising that many Americans now believe that I. G. Farben Industrie means Imperial German Color Industry. But those familiar with that awful German language know that the abbreviated I. G. Farben really means *Interessen Gemeinschaft Farbenindustrie Aktiengesellschaft*. Old Mark would have shuddered at this name since the Germans use three long words—*Interessen, Gemeinschaft, Aktiengesellschaft*—to convey what the English mean by *Ltd.* and the Americans by *Inc.* But Mark never saw it because he died in 1910 and I. G. Farben was not organized until 1926 when the German dye companies, which had been making dyes for half a century or so, were pulled together into a giant combine which hoped to regain the position that Germany had in dyes prior to World War I.

That position was a formidable one—a position every businessman would like to have. Germany, at the start of World War I towered above all competitors in dyes like a giant oak tree in a wheat field. There were thirteen major dye firms in Germany and a dozen or so lesser ones and they all were good at it.

Five of the thirteen majors had been formed for the express purpose of making dyes and the rest were older German chemical firms which had gone into dyes during the dye explosion. The five companies formed to make dyes are shown below with the dates of their founding:

Meister Lucius and Bruning	1862
Bayer Co.	1862
Badische Aniline and Soda Manufacturing Co.	1865
Casella and Co.	1870
Berlin Company for Aniline Manufacture	1873

New dye plants were being built throughout the period from 1860 to 1910 but the manufacturers were never able to keep up with the chemists who kept on discovering new individual dyes and whole new classes of dyes, right up until the outbreak of war in 1914.

The English also were busy with their new dyes and new plants but they were far behind the Germans by 1914. Perkin and Son was, of course, the first English dye manufacturer, in 1857, but soon there were others: Simpson, Maule and Nicholson; Read Holliday and Sons; I. Levinstein, Ltd.; British Alizarin; Claus and Ree, and some other smaller dye makers. Many of these firms combined to form British Dyestuffs Corporation in 1919, and then changed in 1927 to Imperial Chemical Industries, Ltd. This was soon shortened to ICI, a name the corporation still uses today.

Some dye manufacturers also had, by 1914, started up in Switzerland, France, Italy, Russia, Spain, Czechoslovakia, Argentina, and Japan but none of them, except perhaps Switzerland, amounted to much. Even the United States had several tiny plants making dyes, the largest being Schoelkopf Aniline and Chemical works at Buffalo, New York.

The British, before World War I, were self-sufficient in dyes and could supply a good basic diet to feed the needs of their dye customers. They also supplied substantial amounts of dyes to their dominions and sold some to foreign countries, including the United States.

But the Germans set before the United States and the rest of the non-British world a banquet of dyes that caused the mouths of dye users to water. The German display of dyes was something any supplier would love to have; it created appetites the customers never knew they had until they saw what the Germans had to offer. While the British characteristically offered a solid meal of boiled meat and potatoes, the Germans had everything from caviar and truffles to filet mignon, roast turkey, lobster thermidor, venison, oysters on the half shell, baked Alaska, and cherries jubilee with after dinner cigars.

Even that awful German language did not hold back the German dye salesman offering such a display of products. A salesman with the most and best of nearly everything can still make a sale even if he ends his sentences with verbs, prepositions, adjectives, or dangling participle phrases.

The French, Russian, and Italian dye manufacturers offered a few regional dishes such as borscht and spaghetti but they provided the Germans no real competition. The Americans, in their few tiny dye plants, did not produce enough product to sprinkle on a main dish for seasoning purposes.

Consequently, when the British clamped a blockade on Germany late in 1914 the United States became the most dye-starved nation in the civilized world.

Now it might seem, since Britain then ruled the oceans, that the British had an ideal opportunity to pick up the American dye business and run away with it. But the British could not—for two reasons.

First, because the British were locked in a grim life-and-death struggle and had to spend all their efforts on war supplies, they could not expand their dye plants. The war, which had been expected to last a few months when the guns of August sounded in 1914, had settled into a trench war stalemate that consumed gunpowder and men in awful quantities. So the British poured everything into munitions work but even so could not keep up with the demand for gunpowder. Second, the British simply did not know how to make many of the dyes the Germans had used to whet the appetites of their customers.

The United States could not obtain even the dyes which it had been using to print stamps, and eosin was in such short supply that bookkeepers had to change their long-established practice of showing losses in red ink. There was no red ink available.

This situation got worse and worse as the war dragged on and the few submarine loads of dyes that the Germans sneaked by the British blockade just frustrated the Americans and made them more eager than ever for the feast of dyes to which they had once been accustomed.

This, then, was the situation when the Du Pont Company decided it would go into the dye business to fill a national need—and to make some money. There was an almost frantic demand for dyes but Du Pont and other American companies, such as National Aniline and Grasselli Chemical which went into dyes at about the same time, knew that it would be a difficult job.

They all had very little practical "know how" about dye manufacture. Furthermore, they were aware that sooner or later the war would end and they would face competition from Germans who had had half a century of production experience and were supported by the findings of skilled chemists who had given two or three thousand man-years of attention to an arcane branch of chemistry about which most Americans knew nothing.

FIRST ATTEMPTS— SULFUR COLORS AND INDIGO

4

When the Du Pont Company decided in 1917 to enter the dye business it made two wise decisions. One was to locate the new dye works at Deepwater, New Jersey, and the other was to start manufacture with sulfur colors and indigo.

The Deepwater location had several advantages. It was just across the Delaware River from Wilmington and therefore could receive generous attention from the central management. Also it was located just north of the point where Salem Creek flowed into the salty water of the Delaware River, and by putting a dam across the Creek the plant could be assured of a good supply of fresh water. Finally and most importantly, the Du Pont research center, Eastern Laboratory, was located only a few miles up the Delaware at Gibbstown so technical assistance was readily available. It was soon clear that technical assistance was what the new plant needed more than anything else.

The sulfur colors represented the closest thing there was in the dye field to cookbook chemistry. That is to say, the people who made sulfur colors did not know the chemical formulas for the dyes they were making. Nor did the Germans. They simply heated certain materials with sulfur or sulfur-containing chemicals and hoped for the best. That was the case in 1917 and it is still the case today. Dye chemists do not know how to write the formula for sulfur colors. They can prove that these dyes contain certain chromophores, but just how these chromophores are hooked together or what the molecular weight of the dye is no one can say. This is partly because a given batch of a sulfur color may contain several hundreds of different chemical entities, not just half a dozen or so as was the case for Perkin's Mauve and Bismarck Brown.

Du Pont decided to start with sulfur black for two reasons. First, it was assumed, quite erroneously, that it would be the easiest sulfur color to make since black was a good mixture of all other shades, and second because the sulfur blacks were made by reacting sulfur polysulfide with dinitro phenol, a chemical that Du Pont was familiar with from its work on the explosive trinitro phenol, which also went under the name of picric acid.

Despite the widespread ignorance about sulfur colors, they had been around as commercial products for several decades in 1917 and the beginning point for them was almost as old as Perkin's mauve.

This beginning point is another example of how a shrewd analysis of unexpected results from an unplanned experiment can lead to something useful in chemistry. In 1860 an unidentified chemist tried to clean up a spill of sodium sulfide by absorbing it on sawdust, and noticed that the resulting slurry stained cotton cloth. He had made a sulfur color. But nothing was done about it commercially until about 1870 when two chemists got a patent on the making of dyes for cotton by heating various materials containing cellulose, such as sawdust, with sodium polysulfide. They sold their product under the name of *Cachou de Laval*.

It was the first commercial sulfur color but it was a very poor one, and it was not until about 20 years later, after the triaryl methane and azo dyes had become sensations, that sulfur colors really took off.

The Germans found that they could get better control of the shade of color produced if they started with identifiable chemicals rather than mixtures such as were found in trees, weeds, and similar living materials. It was then that sulfur colors became large volume items in the dyeing of textile fibers. Also, the Germans found that they got better control of the reactions if they used water solutions of sodium polysulfide instead of just baking their starting materials with dry sulfur. Even so the new dyes varied greatly in hue, from batch to batch, and they were always dull in shade compared to the triaryl methane dyes and most of the azo dyes. They were sold mostly as browns, yellows, oranges, and blacks and no one knew how to make a red sulfur color. But they were cheap and reasonably fast to washing. Interest in the sulfur colors peaked around 1910 and their use was declining by 1917, but the shortages caused by the war made any kind of dye much sought after in the United States.

Construction of the new dye works in what had recently been a farm on the New Jersey side of the Delaware, which was only slightly above sea level, was pushed with great vigor, once the decision had been made to go ahead. Soon the young engineers in charge were ready to make a batch of sulfur black even though the roads connecting the power plant and the manufacturing unit had not been finished and there was mud everywhere. The rush was due in part to the belief that soon the war would be over and competing dyes from Europe would then be available once more. There would surely be a lot of resentment against the Germans but experienced businessmen were aware that customers soon learn to control their resentments if they can get a better product at the same price or the same product at a lower price.

Now those who are not "skilled in the art," as patent chemists say, might think that it would be impossible to fail in making a sulfur black. The uninitiated might think that even soot from the smoke stack of the power plant could be dumped in with the dye and no one would know the difference.

Alas, this was far from the truth, as the young engineers running those first production attempts soon found out. Some of those first batches of sulfur black had deficiencies they had never even dreamed about. The "dye" they produced could not be dissolved, or if it could be dissolved it would not attach itself to cotton. Also, sometimes the materials in the reaction vessel, which did not have good agitation or heat control instruments, got overheated and boiled out on the floor of the building where it seemed to be quite compatible with the mud which was everywhere.

A longer lasting problem was the fact that sulfur black was not just a black. It came in various shades of red and green and they never knew what shade they were going to produce in any given batch. Again, it might not seem to the uninitiated that a textile dyer would care whether his cloth came out looking black with a reddish cast to it or with a greenish cast, but they did.

In 1917 a great amount of clothing was assembled in sweat shops with women sewing the two sleeves on a shirt using right arm sleeves that came from one source and left arm sleeves from another. And even the poorest customer did not like it if the two sleeves on his one shirt did not look the same shade. So dyers wanted to buy dyes which matched a standard so they could bid on either one or both sleeves when the sweat shop owner came to them. But matching a standard—any standard, red or green shade—was one of the many things which the young engineers at the new dye works could not do.

So Dr. Elmer Bolton, director of Du Pont's central research organization was called over to the dye works to offer expert advice. Unfortunately, he didn't know any more about making sulfur black than the young engineers so he asked Dr. Harold Elley, a young Ph.D. fresh from college, and then working up at the Gibbstown explosives laboratory, to come down and help the engineers solve their problem.

Alas, Dr. Elley knew no more about how to solve the problems than Dr. Bolton did. For one thing, there were dozens of problems, not just one.

Dr. Elley decided to make a study of the available literature on sulfur colors, but this literature consisted mostly of patents which the Germans had obtained to protect their inventions. Most of the patents had expired and with the war still on even the live patents could be used anyway—if they could be understood. But the patents were masterpieces of obfuscation.

A patent is a grant by the government to an inventor giving him exclusive use of what he has invented for a fixed period of time—seventeen years in the United States. In return for this grant, the inventor is required to disclose what he has discovered so that after the seventeen years are up, other people can freely use the information. In this way inventors are encouraged to make discoveries and society, in the long term, also benefits from these discoveries.

If the inventor does not choose to disclose what he has discovered he can, of course, continue to make use of his invention exclusively for as long as he can keep it a secret. But if the secret gets out then everyone can use it freely because the government will not then give him a patent. The patent system has a stick and a carrot attached to it.

But inventors, like most other people, would like to have their cake and eat it too so they usually try to take out patents on their inventions but also try to write their discoveries so other people cannot learn from the patent exactly what they have been doing. This way their exclusive position can be maintained for longer than seventeen years.

However, the patent office of the government tries to make sure that when it makes a grant, called a "claim," the inventor has fully disclosed the information needed to support this claim. So the inventor tries to claim as much as he can hope to get away with, and to disclose as little as possible of the practical details that tell how the process works. The battle between the government and inventors has been going on ever since the patent system began. Inventors not only do not want to disclose fully what their invention consists of but they frequently try to "claim" inventions which were really invented by others at an earlier date.

An example will make it clear how inventors try to make their claims as wide as possible and their disclosures as small as possible.

Let us assume that a grape farmer discovers that if he sprays his ripe grapes with wine the robins will no longer eat them. He can do this secretly and have an advantage over his competitors but if a disgruntled farmhand takes his secret to other farmers he has lost his advantage. So he decides to take out a patent on his new discovery. This way he can prevent his competitors from spraying their vineyards, or force them to pay him a royalty if they do.

So this unsophisticated farmer writes a patent application, in plain English, which says "I have found that spraying ripe grapes with wine will keep the robins from eating them," and "I claim the process of spraying grapes with wine to prevent the robins from eating them."

Good. But a more sophisticated farmer might suspect that a dilute solution of bourbon or even vodka would work just about as well. Also, the grape farmers in the next county may not be bothered by robins but find that bluebirds or cardinals are eating their grapes. So he writes his patent application this way: "I have found that spraying ripe grapes with a dilute solution of ethyl alcohol will keep songbirds from eating them," and "I claim the process of spraying grapes with a dilute solution of ethyl alcohol to protect them from songbirds."

Better. But a veteran farmer might expand his disclosures to include birds of all kinds and fruits of all sorts so that even peach farmers would have to pay him a royalty if eagles attacked his peaches and he sprayed them with ouzo to protect his crop.

Much better. But even the greenest patent attorney would advise the farmer to expand his disclosures and claims to cover all kinds of alcohols, from methanol to decanol, and all kinds of fruits and vegetables so that if these fruits and vegetables were attacked by any flying thing, from fruit flies to buzzards, other farmers would have to pay him a royalty.

This kind of thing can be carried too far because all the disclosures must work, at least to a small extent, or no claim will be granted. And if the patent examiner believes the disclosures are being padded so that other people cannot really learn what is truly effective he may insist that it all be condensed. Consequently, even the most aggressive patent attorney would not try to write disclosures and claims which would protect Norway pines and date palms from attack by dodo birds, petrodactyls, and other extinct species, on the grounds that these species may, sometime in the future, come back to life. But he might try to include flying fish, and jumping frogs on the grounds that they both travel through the air and might develop a taste for peaches or grapes.

Anyway, the Germans had long ago established themselves as masters in the field of writing patents on dyes and all the world has tried to emulate them ever since. So Dr. Elley and his young associates found nothing in the patents to explain the startling results obtained when they first began to make sulfur black. If a charge boiled out of the reaction vessel it sometimes was possible to go back to the patents and find an obscure hint that indeed this might occur if a certain action was taken, or not taken, but this hint was recognizable only after the event had occurred.

Dr. Elley knew that what he needed was advice from someone who had seen, firsthand, how the Germans made sulfur black. So he decided to visit Dr. Gellert Alleman, professor of chemistry at nearby Swarthmore College, since Dr. Alleman had studied chemistry in Germany for a few years, as was the custom for nearly all American chemists in those days.

Alas again, Dr. Alleman knew a lot about what the Germans were doing in general in the field of organic chemistry but not much about dyes. However, he offered Dr. Elley a German book on dyes, but alas one final time, this book had only a paragraph or two on sulfur black. These paragraphs were about as useful as two paragraphs would be to a farmhand who was given the thirty thousand separate pieces which are used in assembling an automobile and told to use them in putting together a car.

So the struggle at the dye works continued mostly by trial and error. In a few months the young engineers began to make some sulfur black which could be sold—so long as there was no competition from Europe. But then the war ended and sulfur black from Europe, mostly Germany, began to be available again and the dye works was again in trouble. The imported material was more consistent in shade, solubility, and dyeing properties—most of the time but not always.

Also chemists began to come from Germany who claimed to be experts in the manufacture of dyes. They were fleeing from the chaos in Germany that had been caused by four years of bitter war, followed by impossible conditions of reparations imposed on Germany by the victorious allies, and finally a runaway inflation which was far worse than the world had ever seen before.

These chemists all claimed to be experts and some of them were. Others were braggarts and frauds. The Du Pont Company hired some of both types.

One of the frauds was an aggressive fellow who claimed he knew all there was to know about making sulfur black, but when he was given a free hand to show what he could do, the color he produced in the plant was as variable as it had ever been. One batch was even greener in shade than anything the young engineers had made. Whereupon the fraud claimed he had produced a new superior quality of sulfur black and if the sales division could not sell it then he would be glad to. And he did. But the next batch was redder than the old standard so once more he went through his act and also sold it. After a few more flip-flops it became apparent to all that the fraud was a fraud and he departed to work for a competitor, claiming to know how they made sulfur black in Germany and at Du Pont.

Two genuine experts who came over from Germany in the early years of sulfur colors were Dr. Englemann and Dr. Runge. They and some of their American associates finally straightened out the manufacture of sulfur black. One of the devices they used was the blending of red and green shade batches to produce a mixture that was close to the standard that had been set up. This grinding, mixing, and blending operation later became a general procedure at the dye works. In a few years a separate area of the plant became known as the "grinding and mixing area." Here most of the dyes were blended to match their standards. Only a few very pure dyes, such as Crystal Violet and Rhodamine B, were sold without having to blend batches which, standing alone, were on one side or the other of the standard. This was one of the practical details not disclosed in the German patents but most inventors would argue that this sort of thing was something that anyone "skilled in the art" would understand. So don't tell them but give them the exquisite pleasure of learning it the hard way.

The need for technical assistance at the dye works became more and more urgent as new dyes were added to the list and in 1921 a new research center, Jackson Laboratory, was built at the plant site. In two decades it became perhaps the greatest center for research on organic chemicals, particularly dyes, in the world.

Dr. Englemann stayed at the dye works for a number of years and became something of a legend because of his knowledge of dyes and his air of great self-confidence. He walked down the corridors of Jackson Laboratory like a Prussian baron, taking the center of the road for himself and extending his elbows to make sure no one crowded him. From time to time his superiors in the organization sent him letters they received asking for information in his fields of interest. Dr. Engleman was not flattered by this deference to his knowledge and often delayed answering such letters on the grounds that they were a nuisance which might go away if ignored for a few weeks or months.

One such letter, however, was deemed important by his superiors and when they were unable to prod Dr. Englemann into making a reply they asked his secretary to help stir him into action.

"Where is this letter?" he asked when she brought the matter to his attention. The secretary went to the files, obtained the letter and gave it to Dr. Englemann. He looked at it briefly and then tore it into small pieces.

"Now there is no letter to answer," he said. However, despite this incident and others like it, the proud Prussian did much to advance the development of workable processes for new dyes.

One of these new dyes, indigo, was started up with relative ease, compared to the sulfur blacks, and remained in the Du Pont product line for about thirty years. This was partly because indigo was a well defined chemical entity for which an exact formula could be written, and partly because the people at the dye works were beginning to become skilled in the art of making dyes. Just beginning.

Du Pont indigo was not the first indigo produced in America. This dye is one of the oldest known to man and it was being isolated from living plant sources in India, from which the name was derived. It was also produced in Africa and China before Columbus set sail for America. A great many different kinds of plants produce indigo so it surely serves some useful biological purpose for plants. In India, plants of the indigofera series produce it, in China the polygonum tinctorium plant makes it, and in Europe the woad plant, isatis tinctoria, also makes indigo. The woad plant was grown in North Carolina and Georgia during the period from 1750 to about 1850 but this industry died out after the Civil War when the dye was imported from India more cheaply than it could be grown in the South. After the Germans learned how to make it from aniline, the growing of plants to produce indigo died out all over the world except perhaps for a few remote villages in China, Africa, and Asia Minor.

The Germans, in fact, developed several processes for making indigo in the laboratory but all of them involved the benzene derivative, aniline, and the best one used sodamide in a hot fusion step. It was the process used at the dye works.

Whenever chemists are inclined to throw out their chests and declare themselves to be geniuses they should give some thought to the fact that indigo plants have been making indigo for countless thousands of years. And that little shellfish, murex brandaris, has been making dibromo indigo, the famous tyrian purple so much prized by ancient kings for the collars of their royal robes, for probably just about as long. Indigo was once the largest volume dye of them all and it still is used in blue jeans and other high fashion items, but by the time chemists learned how to make that tyrian purple, dibromo indigo, in the laboratory there was not much demand for it. Kings became scarce after World War I and the few who remained on their thrones developed a taste for less gaudy colors.

Not only can vegetables and poor fish make complicated dyes which baffled the chemists for many years, but even today a two month old indigo plant and a baby shellfish can make their special dyes far more simply than chemists can. The vegetable and the poor fish work at low temperatures (never above about 40°C) while chemists have to heat their reaction vessels to 200° or 300°C and blast their reactants with such corrosive things as molten sodium hydroxide and sodamide.

As already noted, indigo remained on the Du Pont list of dyes for over a quarter of a century and during that time made some modest profits. However, perhaps the most important thing about indigo was that it caused sodium to be introduced to the dye works.

During the half century after 1920 more than eight billion pounds of sodium were consumed at the dye works, or the Chambers Works as it came to be called later on. Very little of this huge amount of sodium was used to make indigo and over 95% of it was used in the production of tetra ethyl lead, a volatile liquid used as an additive for gasoline to improve its antiknock properties. Tetra ethyl lead, as will be seen, became important to the profitability of dyes, indirectly, both during the period from 1940 to 1965, when dyes were highly profitable, and also after 1965 when dyes began the downhill slide that led to the sale of the business in 1980.

During most of this period from 1920 to 1965 the head keeper of sodium, so to speak, was Edgar W. Fielding, one of the legends of the dye works.

KEEPER OF
THE SODIUM

5

odium is an enigmatic metal. It is a mild looking lemon-colored material that is soft enough to be cut with a dull knife, like a stick of butter in cold but not freezing weather. But if a lump of sodium is thrown into water it starts acting like an enraged dragon spitting out flashes of orange and blue fire and exploding in all directions. The residue, after the fireworks end, consists of sodium hydroxide, a very corrosive material to human flesh.

The use of sodium at Du Pont's dye works began in 1918 when indigo manufacture started there and sodium was needed to make the sodamide required for one step in manufacture of the dye. This particular use of the metal never became a large one, but consumption of sodium increased rapidly after the dye works began to manufacture tetra ethyl lead (TEL) for use as an antiknock additive in gasoline. By 1950 the plant was consuming over a hundred million pounds of sodium per year and it was shipped in tank cars from Niagara Falls where it was made by the electrolysis of salt. During all this time no one was seriously injured by this enigmatic dragon of a metal because it was always kept under control and away from exposure to water.

The man who was responsible, more than any other one person, for this remarkable safety record was Ed Fielding who was about as much of an enigma as sodium itself.

Ed Fielding, keeper of the sodium, is seated closest to the camera. The man with the mustache, on his left, is Jim Reed, the other half of the famous team of Fielding and Reed. This party honoring Stan Ford, the Azo color expert, is unique in that wives were included.

Fielding's deeply lined, craggy face and thin white hair made him look aged when he was only 35 or 40 years old, but behind this solemn mask of a face there lurked a personality better suited to a college sophomore than to a production manager responsible for the activities of a thousand or so chemical workers. In fact, "college sophomore" is probably too sedate and elderly a term to describe him because Fielding was more like a schoolboy—a Tom Sawyer always ready to heave a dead cat into the classroom just to see how much commotion it would create.

While there was in him an undeniable urge to create nondestructive mischief, he kept it under tight control just as he kept sodium under tight control. It was an article of faith in the Du Pont Company that not only was it possible to run any chemical operation safely but that it must be done that way, and no one preached this gospel more consistently and effectively than Ed Fielding. He took great pride in the fact that the inherently hazardous operations that he managed were also safe ones.

"Our operators are much safer at work than they are at home," he boasted, and the record bore him out. Time-losing injuries from work hours were consistently only about a tenth as numerous as those incurred at home, despite the fact that Fielding managed some of the most hazardous operations at the dye works—things such as the production and use of hydrofluoric acid for "Freon" refrigerants, the use of sodium in tetra ethyl lead manufacture, and the even touchier use of sodamide in indigo production.

Ed Fielding was a fiercely competitive man—so competitive that when he went to see a football game he simply had to have a bet on some outcome of the game. If none of his companions was willing to bet on one of the two teams involved, he would bet that one end of the field would have more points scored there than at the other end. He usually tried to obtain a small advantage by choosing the goal line which was downwind, but if necessary he would take the other end. Challenge and tension were things he loved to encounter and this is perhaps one reason why sodium was of more interest to him than most of the chemicals he worked with. It might blow up—but not if he kept it under tight control. So he always seemed to be fascinated by it.

Edgar Wayne Fielding was born in 1894 in the Oklahoma Territory where his father was a territorial judge, who came to Oklahoma shortly after the grand wagon rush that occurred when the Territory was officially opened for settlement by white men. Young Ed graduated from the University of Oklahoma in 1914 and while there developed a lifelong addiction to college football. While he was not qualified to be called a "Sooner," in the original meaning of having jumped the gun announcing the opening of the Territory for settlement, he was one of the most dedicated fans of Sooner football during the period when Coach Bud Wilkinson was either winning national championships or threatening to do so year after year.

In those years Fielding bet Oklahoma against anyone who wanted to back his own alma mater against the Sooners. The various colleges he bet against did not have to play Oklahoma; the Fielding challenge called for total points scored by Oklahoma against total points scored by the opposing bettor's school, with ten cents being paid for each point in the difference between the two totals. Oklahoma usually played a ten-game schedule in those days while most other colleges played only nine but this handicap did not deter his opponents because he always held a "victory dinner" for his opponents after the football season ended and it was always a rip-roaring good party.

One year Fielding won over nine hundred dollars and was hard put to spend it all on one party but he did, with lobsters, steaks, and silver ashtrays for all. One of his opponents that year was a University of Virginia man who had threatened to back out of his bet when Virginia went scoreless for three consecutive games. He did not carry out this threat but when the steaks and lobsters were served at the victory banquet, this aristocrat from below the Mason-Dixon line was served last and what he received was a small bacon, lettuce, and tomato sandwich. After the laughter died out, Fielding gave the waiter a signal and a lobster replaced the sandwich.

This was one side of the man who was in charge of sodium when it first came to the dye works and who kept it under control for nearly half a century. There were many other sides.

Fielding did not come to Du Pont directly from the University of Oklahoma but first spent a year in graduate work at the University of Chicago. He was employed by Du Pont's Experimental Station on the Brandywine River in 1916.

"I reported for work at 8:00 a.m., January 1, 1916," he said, "but was astonished to find the gates were closed with no sign of life anywhere. There wasn't even a guard at the gate. It never occurred to me that New Year's Day was a holiday for these effete Easterners. In Oklahoma the first of January was as much a work day as the first of February. But I learned fast and that was the last time I ever showed up for work on January 1."

Fielding was promptly shipped off to Niagara Falls where sodium was being produced in commercial quantities and then returned to the dye works as a certified expert on sodium.

"I learned at Niagara that sodium is easy to deal with if it is kept away from water but is a real tiger if it gets wet," he once said, while talking about his early experience with sodium. "Actually," he went on, "the first time I ever saw any sodium my high school chemistry teacher said he would show us how it caught fire if placed in water but when he put a small piece in a beaker of water it didn't do a thing. I think he had kept it around so long the air had converted it all to sodium oxide, but at the time it was a great mystery to us all. Later on in college, the freshmen used to amuse themselves by throwing small pieces in the sink where it usually produced a brief fireworks display. It was a lot of fun until one day someone put a big piece in the sink. It went down the drain and blew the gooseneck halfway through the floor below it."

He paused in his story and a quick smile, a half grin, flashed across his solemn face, like summer lightning on a dark night, then he added: "They never found out who threw that big piece of sodium in the sink, but actually it wasn't really so big after all—about twice the size of a lima bean."

Fielding said that he was still a little nervous about handling sodium when he began production of indigo, but by the time TEL manufacture started at the dye works he was quite at ease with it.

Sodium was reacted with lead, on an atom-for-atom basis, to make lead-sodium alloy and this alloy was reacted with an excess of ethyl chloride to produce TEL. Only small quantities of TEL were produced at first but it quickly proved to be the best antiknock compound ever discovered for improving the octane rating of gasoline. Soon it was being produced in million pound quantities, even though only a cubic centimeter or two was required to treat a gallon of gasoline.

"We first got sodium in the form of bricks," Fielding said. "Next it came in drums and finally it came in tank cars, most of which crossed the Delaware River in railroad barges, for some strange reason known only to the railroad lines. I often wondered what would happen if one of those tank cars toppled overboard when a big wave hit the barge. I had a good idea, because in the middle twenties someone began to toss chunks of sodium into the river every now and then when the company ferryboat was returning workers to Wilmington at the end of the day shift. The sodium danced around and made some small explosions but never caused any real excitement until one night when everyone rushed to one side to see what was the matter and almost capsized the ferry. Mr. Porch was the plant manager then and he was no dummy. He called me into his office the next day and said he was sure the incident was caused by someone throwing sodium over board. 'It has to be someone in your organization, Ed,' he said, 'so I want you to get the word down the line that if it happens again I'm going to find out who did it and fire him. That kind of thing is horseplay and we won't tolerate it.' I told Mr. Porch that I would see to it that it never happened again and it never did." This time the quick flash of a smile was even briefer than it usually was when Fielding was describing his adventures with sodium.

By 1950 TEL was the largest volume product being produced at the plant and was earning more money than all of the dyes combined. The name of the plant had been changed to the Chambers Works, in honor of Dr. Arthur Chambers, who had been one of the early research managers of the organic chemicals department. Fielding was general superintendent of the TEL-"Freon" areas while Jim Reed was general superintendent of all the dyes and chemicals areas.

However, indigo still remained as a part of Fielding's half of the plant while all the other 500 or so dyes were under Reed, so one day one of Fielding's subordinates said: "Ed, why don't you turn indigo over to Jim Reed and get out of the dye business?".

"For several reasons," Fielding replied. "First, indigo isn't making any money to speak of and Jim Reed doesn't want it. Second, the indigo building is located at my end of the plant and third, I couldn't get out of the dye business if I tried. I'm carrying over half of the overhead on the plant and still two or three percent of the dyes are losing money. If it weren't for TEL and "Freon," 15 or 20 percent of all dyes would be losing money."

This matter of the distribution of overhead costs was a source of argument that lasted throughout the history of the dye works and continued after it became known as the Chamber Works. The dyes superintendents always claimed they were charged too much in overhead while the superintendents of TEL, "Freon," and heavy chemicals claimed that dyes did not carry enough overhead. The argument sometimes extended up the line organization to the general manager, but most general managers avoided it on the grounds that no matter how overhead was charged it would not increase profits for the department. Most but not all ignored it; some studied it at length and in vain.

These arguments sometimes generated bitter feelings but never between Fielding and Reed who got along together famously. They even formed a joint master-of-ceremonies team which probably has never been equalled in the Du Pont Company.

In those days employees were encouraged to hold dinners to celebrate occasions such as retirements, promotions, transfers to new locations, and long service anniversaries. The theory was that these dinners promoted good fellowship among the employees and thus led to better cooperation among the various groups in the plant—resulting in greater productivity.

Sometimes this was true. But on other occasions the dinners were enormously boring affairs which irked all who attended them. This seemed to be the case for retirement parties in particular. Those presiding at the retirement parties often suffered from the belief that they were expected to say something profound and to praise the man retiring in gross and extravagant language for hours on end.

Albee Williams, when he was superintendent of the Basic Colors Area, came back from a retirement party and said that "Walt's party set a new low for retirements. We had seven speakers and each one of them felt compelled to reproduce every cliché he had ever heard of. One of them had Walt coming into his golden years, another had him in his sunset years, another in his twilight days and so on and on until it was nearly ten-thirty before poor Walt was called on to reply. He was almost in tears by then and in a few minutes he actually was as he proceeded to thank each speaker in such mournful terms that soon the entire audience was weeping or asleep. By the time Walt finished it was after eleven o'clock."

And it often happened that way at the dye works parties for employees until Reed and Fielding decided that some changes should be made. They believed that such parties should be brief—not over an hour after dessert was served— and they should be fun for all involved, the guest of honor and all those who came to honor him. Their first performance as joint masters of ceremonies was a smashing success and they were besieged with requests for repeat appearances.

It seems to be a fact of history that comedy teams are most effective if the partners are quite different in style— Abbott and Costello, Laurel and Hardy, Burns and Allen, Martin and Lewis, Reed and Fielding.

Fielding's lined, craggy, solemn face reminded his audience of Casey Stengel, the old baseball manager, but there the similarity ended. Casey got his humor and ideas across in a torrent of confused language, but Fielding used words carefully and sparingly in the manner of Mark Twain, who was his favorite author. He realized, as did Mark Twain, that timing is essential to humor and his eloquent pauses often gave his audience a chance to run ahead with their own ideas as to what was coming next. Then they exploded with laughter when he hit them with a surprise—often a single word— all the while giving no indication, except for a rare display of that fleeting half smile/half grin, which was his trademark, that what he was saying was intended to be funny.

Reed, on the other hand, had a merry dancing pair of eyes set in a mobile face which often exploded into laughter along with his audience. He spoke easily and fluently without *ahs* and *ers,* and never began his monologue with, "This reminds me of the story about. . . ." Instead he got down to business promptly and wove his jokes into the body of his talk so that the audience was never aware that a joke was coming up until suddenly it was upon them. And always the joke was pertinent to the career of the man being honored. Reed's comments were never saccharine; they had acid sprinkled all over them but somehow he kept the acid from stinging the guest of honor although others present might not fare so well.

Reed and Fielding became so much in demand for retirement, anniversary, promotion, and transfer parties that in a plant of ten thousand people they would have had time for little else since the job they did must have required a lot of preparation. So they limited their joint appearances, but even so, they had a profound effect on dye works parties for employees. These parties became shorter, funnier, and more enjoyable for all.

A Reed-Fielding affair, authentic or copied by others, really did promote good employee relations. Cooperation between the dye areas under Reed and the TEL–"Freon" areas under Fielding reached a new high because both Reed and Fielding were masters of psychology. Fielding got his results quietly with few words while Reed got his explosively but both were extremely effective in reaching their goals of high productivity going hand-in-hand with job safety.

Fielding, in particular, knew how to work with indi-

viduals as well as with large audiences and he handled all
ranks with equal effectiveness.

After he was promoted from the Chambers Works to
production manager, with an office in Wilmington, one of his
assignments was to find a new plant site in Texas to which
TEL could be shipped by tanker for blending into motor and
aviation mixes for distribution in that part of the country.
The new plant was also to serve as the first production unit
for "Hypalon," a new synthetic rubber discovered by Jackson
Laboratory. After options to buy had been obtained on the
land Fielding and representatives of the real estate and engineering departments studied it carefully several times, then
they prepared a project to buy the plant site.

At this point the assistant general manager of Orchem, Dr. Samuel Lenher, who later became a senior vice-
president of Du Pont, decided that he too should look at the
site personally before the company spent several million dollars to buy it. Lenher outranked Fielding by several grades
so a trip to Beaumont was arranged, even though Fielding
did not think it was necessary since he had already tramped
over the land four or five times.

Accordingly, Fielding hoped that Lenher would make
a brief inspection of the dock area, look across the fields, and
then stop. Lenher, however, had other ideas and he set out
with Fielding in tow, on a walk that seemed to be designed
to cover every acre in the thousand-acre site. After half an
hour of walking Fielding tried to encourage an abridgment
of this inspection tour.

"Do you want to see any more, Sam?" he asked.

"Yes, I do," was the reply. "After all we are going to
ask the company to spend a lot of money here and I want to
be sure there are no hidden problems anywhere in the plant."

So they kept on walking, but Fielding had not given
up.

"We walked a few yards further," he said in telling
about the trip, "and then I said, 'Sam, it is interesting that

we have been walking here in the cottonmouth snake country for half an hour and so far today I haven't seen a single snake.' Sam said nothing and we kept on walking for about a minute. Then he said to me 'Ed, I think I have seen enough of this site. Let's go back to the car and head for our plane.' "

Fielding told this story a number of times but always at the end he paused and that quick smile flashed across his face again. "It was all the simple truth;" he concluded. "I hadn't seen a cottonmouth snake that day—or any other day at Beaumont."

While Fielding's assignment as a production manager took him away from the Chambers Works it didn't take him away from sodium. One day the safety measures which he and his associates had devised to keep sodium under control were put to the supreme test.

Three tank cars filled with sodium were loaded on a railroad barge at Pigeon Point, Delaware, one night waiting to be ferried across the river to the Chambers Works when a fast moving tanker came past the dock. The wake from the tanker caused the barge to tilt past the critical point and all three sodium cars rolled over the side and plunged beneath the waters of the Delaware River. All openings to the cars were sealed so nothing happened but when the railroad notified Du Pont of the incident things then did begin to happen.

The general manager of Orchem was alarmed and so was the director of public relations who began to speculate that if a leak occurred in one of those cars it might rupture, throw a hundred thousand pounds of sodium into the river, and parts of the steel car into downtown Philadelphia. So the director of manufacture and Ed Fielding were dispatched to Pigeon Point to see what could be done. The director of manufacture was beginning to have visions not far removed from those of the director of public relations, but Fielding was undisturbed.

"Don't worry," he said. "We designed those cars to keep sodium safe in a combined railroad wreck and rainstorm.

Dr. Samuel Lenher held many positions in the organic chemicals department, including that of assistant general manager during the period when dyes were highly profitable. Later on he became an executive vice-president of Du Pont and chairman of the board of trustees of the University of Delaware. According to Ed Fielding, keeper of the sodium, Lenher maintained a dignified posture even when threatened by cottonmouth water snakes. (Photograph courtesy Public Affairs Department, E. I. du Pont de Nemours & Company.)

They have double walls made of thick steel and all the openings have a double valve system. Those cars will just sit there until we find a barge with a derrick big enough to lift them out of the river."

And that is the way it all turned out. It took a week or so to find the barge and two days to find the cars because they had settled in the mud which was twenty feet deep in that part of the river. But then they were raised, put back on the railroad barge, and carried over to the Chambers Works where the sodium in them was used in the routine manner for such things.

When it was all over Fielding told the director of manufacture: "See, I told you those cars were accident proof."

Then he paused and said: "It is all too bad in a way. It would have been exciting to see railroad cars leaping out of the water like porpoises."

He had displayed a similar point of view some years earlier following a safety meeting at Chambers Works.

The dye works—Chambers Works—handled literally thousands of flammable materials during the period from 1920 to 1980 and from time to time some of them caught fire, but there was never a fire that threatened to destroy any considerable part of the plant. This was due partly to the industry and courage of the fire chief there, a man with the improbable name of Royden Sparks, but mostly to the almost incredible amount of attention given to matters of safety.

Meetings were held every day by various groups on every aspect of safety including, of course, fires. At one of these meetings the Chief Engineer, Lou Marcotte, was presiding and he had collected all the general superintendents and Chief Sparks to provide expert testimony on all aspects of fires at the plant.

Chief Sparks was not technically trained but he was a man of great good common sense and outstanding courage who had many times quickly extinguished fires that might have otherwise got out of control. The Chief said, among other things, that water was a marvelous firefighter and was very cheap. He said that he had found over the years that the best thing to do with almost any fire was to flood it with water. The water cooled everything down and the clouds of steam tended to shut off the supply of oxygen, thus extinguishing the fire. Everyone agreed that this made good sense, but Marcotte and Fielding added notes of caution. Marcotte said that care had to be used in spraying water on electrical circuits because this might cause short circuits which would start new fires.

Then Fielding said that it was clearly wrong to spray water on a sodium fire because the sodium would react with the water to release hydrogen which would explode and spread the sodium around making the fire worse. A sodium fire must be fought by dumping sand, dry dirt, soda ash, or some other inert material on it.

Chief Sparks said that he knew all this and the meeting broke up. But as those present were leaving Marcotte, who was a shrewd judge of people, walked up to Chief Sparks and said: "Chief, I know you wouldn't spray water on an ordinary sodium fire, but what would you do if we had a big sodium fire? Say one of the storage tanks down at the sodium farm?"

Instantly the Chief shot back: "I'd flood the SOB with water!"

Fielding had gone out of the room before this exchange occurred but when he heard about it, that quick grin crossed his wrinkled face and he said: "It would be a show worth burning half the plant down to see, but one of my young engineers would lasso the Chief and hog-tie him before he got even one hose hooked up and run down to the sodium farm. We don't even have a water line within a hundred yards of it."

BUILD-UP TO CRITICAL SIZE

6

By 1920 the Du Pont Company's dye works at Deepwater, New Jersey was making good sulfur black—most of the time. It never did have much trouble making indigo, aside from a few "boil-overs" and minor problems of that sort, partly because some Du Pont chemists had been given access to a German owned indigo plant in England that had been seized by the British when World War I started. It helped enormously to see a dye plant in actual operation.

However, it was obvious that no manufacturer of dyes would be able to compete during peacetime if it offered only a black and a blue to customers who had been accustomed, before the war, to choose from a whole rainbow of colors such as the Germans had offered. The Germans would surely try to regain their dye business when peace was restored.

Also, it was clear that there would be a large amount of domestic competition because Du Pont was not alone in trying to become a supplier of dyes. Over a hundred American companies, representing an investment of about two hundred million dollars, had been started in order to make dyes in America.

Some of the new firms were small, making only one or two special dyes for which they had somehow obtained the required technology. Others were not basic manufacturers at all but simply did blending and compounding operations.

They might buy several crude dyes from others and then mix and blend them to produce a shade which certain customers had become accustomed to, or they might buy "press cake" and finish it to an ink or a dry dye. A "press cake" was simply a crude dye or pigment which was still wet with water even though most of the water had been pressed out of it.

More than half of these small firms went out of business in the first decade after they got started, some via the bankruptcy route and others by simply giving up when they lost most of their customers. Still others were bought up by larger firms that were trying to reach the critical size that would permit them to survive. However, a few of the small dye and pigment firms which sprang up during, or right after World War I, were still in business in 1950. This was particularly true of small firms which bought press cakes and converted them into inks; they had found a ledge on the mountainside where they could survive by providing a service more cheaply than the larger firms could doing the same thing.

Examples of the larger firms which bought up some of the others were Du Pont, American Cyanamid, and Allied Chemical and Dye Corporation. Some of the companies that were bought up, such as National Aniline and Chemical Co. and the Calco Chemical Company were themselves fairly large in size.

The Du Pont Company went about its program of growth to critical size by a variety of routes. It tried to add individual dyes to its line whenever it could obtain the required technology and soon had built plants to make auramine, safranine (the principal ingredient in Perkin's mauve), eosine, and methyl violet. Du Pont studied the patent literature in search of new dyes but found the patents to be of little help.

The United States government seized all German patents in this country under the Trading-with-the-Enemy Act of 1918 and made them available for licenses. Only 403 licenses were taken out by all Americans from the 4802 patents that had been made available. Not all the 403 licenses were in the field of dyes and some which were, turned out to be useless when they were put into plant practice. Du Pont chemists found them to be generally useless so far as learning how to make a specific dye was concerned. The detailed items of "know-how" were almost never clearly disclosed. If they were given at all they were usually hidden in a welter of irrelevant material so that it was difficult to find the wheat in the vast amount of chaff that came with it. However, reading of the German patents did tend to give American chemists a background for ideas that helped them in subsequent research programs.

Du Pont also tried to obtain technical information from various other sources such as German chemists who had come to the United States trying to escape the chaos of postwar Germany. Some of these people had actually operated dye plants and they carried in their heads many of the practical details needed for successful manufacture of dyes. But sometimes they had forgotten, or never knew, certain critical details and this fact did not become known until sad experience at the dye works made it clear.

Du Pont also purchased a number of the smaller dye firms when it appeared from their performance in the market that these firms knew how to make at least a few high quality dyes. Some of the new acquisitions were not primarily dye manufacturers but did have divisions which made dyes or pigments. These companies were often purchased, at least in part, with Du Pont common stock and since this stock was starting on a period of great appreciation in value, one end result was the creation of a great many new millionaires.

The Grasselli Chemicals Company, purchased in 1928, was primarily a manufacturer of inorganic chemicals such as acids and heavy chemicals, but it did bring with it some dye technology. This was also the case with the Krebs Pigment and Chemical Company, purchased in 1929, and the Commercial Pigments Corporation, acquired in 1931. Krebs produced mostly inorganic pigments but was beginning to get into organic colored materials closely related to dyes. Commercial Pigments was primarily a manufacturer of titanium dioxide but it too had some knowledge of colored organic materials.

Du Pont's most important acquisition in the dye field occurred in 1931 when it bought the dyestuff division of the Newport Company. This acquisition was important because it brought with it people who knew a great amount about all aspects of the dye business—research, manufacture, and sales. The Newport Company had an expertise in the manufacture of anthraquinone dyes which rivaled, and in some cases actually excelled, the Germans. And by 1931 the anthraquinone colors had become the most important of all the high quality cotton dyes. Only the azo dyes sold in larger volume than the anthraquinone or "vat" dyes as they were usually called, but the azos were generally inferior to the vats in light fastness and wash fastness. The term "vat" derived from the fact that the anthraquinone dyes were really insoluble pigments and had to be put in a vat and treated with a reducing agent before they would go in solution and attach themselves to the fiber being dyed.

The Newport Company was of crucial importance because it owned the patent rights and manufacturing "know-how" on Jade Green, the most important of all the vat dyes at that time. Even the Germans could not match Newport's Jade Green in quality, and it was an often repeated joke among the dye works chemists that Du Pont had sold itself to the Newport Company just to get control of Jade Green.

In any event, with acquisition of the Newport anthraquinone dye business, Du Pont had reached critical size. It now knew enough, and had a line of dyes wide enough to permit it to compete both in the United States and in foreign markets. However, it was shooting at moving targets and if Du Pont had stopped in 1931 it would soon have become obsolete. The Germans had recovered to a considerable extent from World War I and were once again adding to their man-years of research in dyes at a faster rate than any other nation.

While manufacturing technology was the most basic need of Du Pont's young dye business throughout the 1920s and 1930s, it was clear even during the 1920s that knowledge of the marketplace was also vital.

The use of dyes was a complex and technical business in its own right, even if not as technical as the manufacturing process. It soon became evident to all the American manufacturers that they would sell more of their dyes if they understood the problems involved in using them in textile mills, paper mills, ink mills, paint mills, and other miscellaneous places. Each expansion of Du Pont's dye business during the 1920's brought some additional knowledge of the market, because customers did not hesitate to make their complaints known.

But this route to expanded knowledge of the market and the problems involved in the use of dyes was a slow and uncertain one and following it seemed likely to cause Du Pont to fall further behind the Germans, instead of gaining on them. So the new organic chemicals department made a very important decision.

It decided to create a special laboratory called the Sales Technical Laboratory with the specific assignment of studying the use of dyes. This laboratory was called "Tech Lab," for short, and it became one of the vital units which permitted Du Pont to reach a critical size in the dye business. It did not merely answer complaints and try to tell customers how to avoid expensive failures in the use of Du Pont dyes. It did research.

Tech Lab embarked on a long series of highly technical studies on the theoretical as well as practical aspects of dyeing. The chemists at Tech Lab delved into the kinetics of dye adsorption and studied many other problems which seemed to have no immediate use but which did increase understanding of the dye process in general.

The information developed by Tech Lab was made available to dye customers by direct contact, by publication in trade and technical journals, and sometimes by patents. These patents attempted what so many previous patents in the dye field had never really tried to do; they tried to make disclosures which were easily understood; they tried to give practical details in simple language. This was not idealism but simply recognition of the fact that customers and competitors should be treated differently.

When Tech Lab's representatives first began to visit customers in the field they often learned more from the customers than the customers learned from them. But as time went by and Tech Lab's researches began to result in the accumulation of a large store of dye expertise this was reversed and representatives of the laboratory were welcomed eagerly whenever they wanted to visit a dye-consuming plant.

Du Pont's investment in the dye business was only about two million dollars in 1920, and the company's long-range plan had called for a total investment of about seven million dollars when the business had grown large enough to be self-supporting. However, this figure had to be raised drastically when it became clear in the late 1920s and early 1930s that the cost of accumulating a critical mass of technical information and production capacity would be far more expensive than originally contemplated.

The dye business lost money during each of its first ten years but turned the corner in 1929, just before the economic crash began, and managed to stay in the black during the worst of the depression years of 1930 to 1934. By 1935 accumulated profits were equal to the total losses of earlier years and the dye business had indeed reached critical size, but the total investment was about $43 million rather than the $7 million originally planned.

All during the buildup period it had become more and more evident that success in the dye business depended on technical knowledge. Some of this knowledge could be purchased and this had been done, as in the case of the Newport vat dye business which brought with it so many dye experts.

These people not only brought with them much accumulated knowledge but they also brought background which permitted them to extend this knowledge by further research.

And this extension was necessary because both the Germans and American competitors were also investing heavily in research. So laboratories became just as important as manufacturing facilities during the 1920s while Du Pont's dye business was struggling to grow. Each area of the expanding dye works found it necessary to install its own laboratory where experimental work to improve yields and quality could be carried out along with control work to maintain existing standards of hue, brightness, solubility, and other required properties. Consequently by the critical size year of 1935 the plant had a whole series of small laboratories such as the Indigo Lab, Sulfur Colors Lab, Basic Colors Lab, Azo Colors Lab, and Naphthalene Intermediates Lab, spread over the thousand acre expanse of the plant.

However, despite the vital importance of Tech Lab and the many small area laboratories, the real keystone of technology for the dye business was the first laboratory built at the dye works, Jackson Laboratory.

7

JACKSON LABORATORY AND THE MACHINE GUNNER

Jackson Laboratory, built at the dye works in 1921, was named in honor of Oscar Jackson, a chemist and expert on explosives who worked at the Repauno Plant a few miles up the Delaware River from Deepwater, New Jersey. Oscar Jackson was the son of Dr. Charles Jackson who had been decorated by King Oscar of Sweden for his work in anesthesia.

After graduating from Harvard in chemistry, Oscar Jackson went to Germany for further study, as all "complete" chemists did in those days. While in Germany he worked with Adolph Bayer the founder of Bayer and Company, one of the first two German companies to begin the manufacture of dyes. Young Jackson did not specialize in dyes, however, and learned little about them because Bayer had other work which interested him more.

After Jackson returned to America he was employed by the Du Pont Company and became an authority in explosives but he was little known outside that field and today very few people have ever heard of him. However, the laboratory named in his honor became known all over the world within two decades after it was founded. This fame resulted partly from scores of minor successes in research but mostly from four products which had become known all over the world: tetra ethyl lead (TEL), neoprene, "Freon" and "Teflon." These four were not only technical success stories but were also highly successful financially.

This astonishing record of achievement by Jackson Laboratory, particularly the record outside the field of dyes which had caused the laboratory to be built, had occurred partly because the Du Pont Company had given its new organic chemicals department a charter of unbelievable dimensions. Organic chemistry includes most of what the world thinks of when it speaks of chemistry today. So the chemists of Jackson Laboratory had been granted the right to explore for Du Pont a field that encompassed about 90% of all chemistry. It was a great opportunity and the chemists of Jackson Laboratory made the most of it. The other reason for the remarkable record of achievement was that these chemists were a remarkable lot.

The first of the products developed by Jackson Laboratory and destined to become known all over the world was TEL. This volatile organic compound of lead had been found by Thomas Midgley and Charles Kettering of General Motors to be a good "antiknock" additive for use in gasoline. That is to say, when a small amount, about a tablespoonful, of TEL was added to a gallon of gasoline, the gasoline burned more efficiently. It did not "knock" and released more energy for a given amount of gasoline.

While Midgley and Kettering knew this they knew next to nothing about how TEL might be produced in the large quantities that would be required if it became widely used in gasoline. Nor did they know if TEL could be manufactured at a cost that would permit it to be used in a product that was as cheap as gasoline was in the 1920s—15 or 20 cents a gallon.

Working first in laboratory equipment and then in a "semiworks," the chemists and engineers of Jackson Laboratory quickly came up with a process which they believed could be scaled-up into a full plant-size operation. This scaleup procedure is not an easy thing, as the dye works chemists had been learning for several years, but for TEL it worked beautifully and the costs were even lower than had been anticipated. It quickly became evident that TEL was, by far, the cheapest of all known processes for increasing the octane rating of a gasoline and thereby reducing its tendency to "knock."

This development of a commercial process for making TEL was carried out with great speed but it sorely tested Du Pont's often stated claim that any chemical process could be operated safely and must be done that way. There were many hazards involved in making TEL—some obvious and some hidden.

It was obvious that the sodium used in making TEL had to be kept out of contact with water or it would release hydrogen and explode. Also, it was obvious that lead and the lead-sodium alloy made from it were poisons that must not be taken into the body, but it was not obvious that TEL itself was an insidiously toxic material. It was a liquid with a rather pleasant sweet odor that apparently did no harm in contact with the skin. It caused no irritation and so seemed harmless. However, the people involved in making TEL soon found that both the liquid and its vapors were serious poisons which caused headaches, vomiting, and severe nerve damage if any significant amount entered the human body. Large quantities caused death in a few hours. All these hazards were guarded against in the full-scale plant but the learning process was a painful one.

One major engineering problem in the large plant was caused by the fact that so much lead metal had to be recycled. A first look at the chemistry involved—reacting ethyl chloride with an alloy of lead and sodium—suggested that four atoms of sodium and one of lead should be reacted with four molecules of ethyl chloride to produce one molecule of TEL, and four molecules of sodium chloride. But when this was tried, practically no TEL was produced. It was found necessary to react one atom of lead with one of sodium and then treat this low sodium alloy with ethyl chloride, but this procedure caused only one-fourth of the lead to be consumed, leaving three-quarters of all the lead to be recycled. It was never possible to avoid this inconvenient fact of life, but eventually the Jackson Laboratory chemists and engineers reduced it to a minimal nuisance value by developing what they called the continuous process for making TEL. That is, they pumped molten lead-sodium alloy into a reactor that was also receiving a continuous stream of hot ethyl chloride. A continuous stream of TEL, excess lead, excess ethyl chloride, and by-product salt came out the other end of the reactor. It was a wicked mixture going in and an even more wicked one coming out the other end of the reactor, but it was done safely, year after year.

During World War II TEL was an item of great military significance because it permitted U. S. aviators to have a higher octane fuel than was available to either German or Japanese pilots. After the war the development of jet planes made TEL obsolete for aviation purposes but it continued to be the most efficient way to obtain high octane ratings for automobile gasolines. Du Pont, and later other suppliers of TEL, made it in billion pound quantities for many years. However, when the pressures for reduced air pollution from automobiles caused General Motors to adopt catalytic afterburners, the use of TEL began to decline sharply because lead from TEL inactivated these catalytic burners and cars had to use lead-free gasoline.

TEL may eventually go the way of the Mississippi steam-boat and coal-fired locomotives but during the half century from 1925 to 1975 it reduced the consumption of crude oil by over ten billion barrels by permitting a more efficient use of gasoline in automobiles.

Neoprene was more nearly a complete Jackson Laboratory development than TEL. Some useful early leads to neoprene came from Father Julius Nieuwland of Notre Dame University and from Dr. Wallace H. Carothers of Du Pont's central research laboratories, but both the invention and development of the process for neoprene took place in Jackson Laboratory.

Neoprene is a synthetic rubber which is vastly superior to natural rubber in resistance to high temperatures, ozone, and oils, and it has continued to find new and expanded uses ever since it was first made available to the public during the early 1930s. The name neoprene, though first used by Du Pont, has become a generic term and refers to any rubber made by the polymerization of chloroprene. It is manufactured in the United States, Germany, Japan, Great Britain, and Russia. Unlike TEL, it has continued to be used in ever-increasing quantities. Neoprene has found so many applications in high technology fields that its future seems secure.

Neoprene also tested Du Pont's belief that all chemical processes can be operated safely, because it started out as a derivative of acetylene, a notoriously treacherous chemical which often explodes for reasons hard to identify. This same touchiness is true for vinyl acetylene which is an intermediate step in the process of going from acetylene to neoprene. Explosions in the manufacture of neoprene caused fatalities on several occasions.

This problem of explosions was not solved until some years after neoprene ceased to be a Jackson Laboratory responsibility. In 1957 the Du Pont Company formally recognized the fact that the organic chemicals department had been given too wide a charter and made a separate department, called the elastomers department, with responsibility for neoprene, "Hypalon," "Viton," and related materials. "Hypalon" and "Viton" were both products which originated in Jackson Laboratory. The new department finally solved the neoprene explosion problem by developing a process that does not use acetylene or vinyl acetylene. However, the neoprene obtained from the new process is still a polymer of chloroprene, just like the original neoprene first made in Jackson Laboratory.

The "Freon" refrigerants are probably better known all over the world than any of the other products invented or developed by Jackson Laboratory during its days of glory. As in the case of TEL, the basic discovery of "Freon" refrigerants did not occur in Jackson Laboratory.

"Freon" 11 and "Freon" 12 were brought to the laboratory in tiny quantities by Dr. A. L. Henne and Dr. Thomas Midgley (the same man who brought those small samples of TEL) and once again the chemists and engineers of Jackson Laboratory were asked if they could develop processes which would produce "Freon" 11 and "Freon" 12 cheaply and in large amounts.

The idea advanced by Midgley was that if "Freon" 12 could be made cheaply it would then be used to make safe air conditioning machines for homes.

Ice had been manufactured for many years employing mechanical refrigeration devices which used refrigerant gases such as ammonia, sulfur dioxide, or propane, and it was obvious that similar machines could be used to air condition houses. However, these machines always allowed some of the refrigerant gas to leak out, sooner or later, and ammonia, sulfur dioxide, and propane were too hazardous to be allowed around a private home. The first two were both toxic and very irritating, while propane could explode if mixed with air. In addition to its toxic and irritating nature ammonia, the most widely used refrigerant in ice making, also could explode when mixed with air.

Midgley and Henne knew that "Freon" 12 was not toxic and could not burn but they also knew that it contained fluorine and would be a difficult material to manufacture on a large-scale basis. "Freon" 12 is difluoro dichloro methane and could be made by reacting methane with chlorine and fluorine but the chemists at Jackson Laboratory found that the best process for making it involved reacting carbon tetrachloride with hydrofluoric acid so that two of the chlorine atoms in the carbon tetrachloride were replaced with fluorine atoms. This sounds simple but it was far from that. Hydrofluoric acid is the most viciously corrosive to human tissue of all acids and to use large quantities of it under pressure required the development of safety precautions which were even more elaborate than those demanded by TEL manufacture.

But all of this was done quickly and soon there was a large-scale plant at the dye works producing "Freon" 11 and "Freon" 12. The modern air conditioning industry began in the early 1930s, as soon as "Freon" 12 became commercially available.

Jackson Laboratory did not stop with the first two "Freon" compounds brought to it by Midgley and Henne. Within a few years a whole series of fluoro chloro compounds had been synthesized and given names by adding numbers after the trademark word "Freon." Many of these chemicals were not commercialized but several were because they had desirable properties not shown by "Freon" 11 and "Freon" 12. Three which became quite important were "Freon" 22, "Freon" 113, and "Freon" 114.

The chemists of Jackson Laboratory developed an intricate code for naming the "Freon" compounds. It was a cryptic system which had no great merit except that it baffled the uninitiated for years. The last number on the right gave the number of fluorine atoms in the molecule. The next digit toward the left was one more than the number of hydrogen atoms in the molecule and the next digit further toward the left was one less than the number of carbon atoms. For example, consider "Freon" 114. The last digit on the right, 4, says that there are 4 fluorine atoms present. The next digit toward the left, 1, is one more than the number of hydrogen atoms, so "Freon" 114 contains no hydrogen. The next digit toward the left, also a 1, is one less than the number of carbon atoms. Thus, "Freon" 114 contains two carbon atoms. One final rule completes the puzzle: Any free valences of carbon not tied–up with hydrogen and fluorine are satisfied by chlorine atoms.

Therefore, "Freon" 114 is tetrafluoro dichloro ethane. Simple!

Two more examples: "Freon" 12 and "Freon" 22. Both of these "Freon" compounds have two fluorine atoms, but

"Freon" 12 has no hydrogen while "Freon" 22 has one hydrogen. Both have only one carbon atom. There is only one carbon in each because the third digit toward the left is missing and one more than nothing is one. "Freon" 12 is difluoro dichloro methane while "Freon" 22 is difluoro monochloro methane, with one hydrogen still left unreplaced in the starting methane. Most people who have devoted their lives to air conditioning have not bothered to learn how to decode the "Freon" puzzle.

When the various "Freon" refrigerants became readily available chemists at Jackson Laboratory and other places found that some of them were useful in fields which had nothing to do with air conditioning. For example, "Freon" 113 was a uniquely useful degreasing solvent, and "Freon" 11 and "Freon" 12 were widely used as propellants in aerosol sprays. These aerosol sprays got started during World War II as insect sprays in the tropics and then became widely used in such items as hair sprays and perfumes.

When the basic patents on the "Freon" chemicals expired other American companies began to manufacture them, using their own trademark names such as "Genetron," "Isotron" and "Ucon". The list of foreign trademarks, given below, indicates how widespread the demand for fluorochloro carbons became during the 1950s and 1960s.

Arcton—England
Daiflon—Japan
Algofrene—Italy
Flurion—Spain
Frigen—West Germany
Frigedohn—East Germany

It irritated other manufacturers to have their products identified as "Freons under another name". However, the Du Pont Company found this habit of consumers to be as alarming as it was flattering because Du Pont did not wish "Freon" to lose its trademark status by becoming known as a generic term, as had happened in the case of neoprene.

Research in the general field of fluorine chemistry, started by the "Freon" products, led to the discovery of "Teflon" which was more clearly a Jackson Laboratory invention than any other of the world famous products already discussed.

Dr. Roy J. Plunkett, a graduate of Manchester College and Ohio State University, was working in the general field of fluorine chemicals and in the course of his work stored some tetra fluoro ethylene in a cylinder, under pressure, for further use at a later time. But when he and his assistant, Jack Rebok, tried to release the tetra fluoro ethylene a week later nothing came from the cylinder. An investigator with less insight, and unaware of how important chance happenings had been to inventors of the past, such as Perkin and his mauve, might have concluded that the cylinder had leaked and its contents had escaped. But Plunkett thought the unsaturated tetra fluoro ethylene might have polymerized and he was right. When the cylinder was cut open he saw a white powdery material.

It was the first "Teflon" anyone had ever seen and Plunkett soon showed that it was a most remarkable product. It resisted nearly all corrosive materials, remained unchanged at temperatures which charred most compounds of carbon, and was extremely slippery.

"Teflon" was carried through only the early stages of development at Jackson Laboratory then was transferred to another department for commercialization, since Du Pont had already seen that the original charter given to the organic chemicals department was far too broad. "Teflon" and its close relative, the heat resistant "Viton" elastomer, also invented at Jackson Laboratory, were vital materials for the space exploration program of the 1970s. Without them the space program might not have been possible. "Viton" is known only to technologists, but "Teflon" has become a household word because of its use in "nonstick" cooking utensils, and Dr. Plunkett has been identified as the chemist "who has done more than anyone else to reduce friction in a world full of tension and strife."

However, despite the four astounding technical and financial successes discussed above and dozens of comparatively minor success stories in such varied fields as surfactants, rubber compounding agents, synthetic camphor, and perfumes, Jackson Laboratory at the end of its second decade was still thought of by most people in Du Pont as a research center for dyes. This view was particularly strong among the chemists who worked there, and by the person most responsible for this view, a man named Ivan Gubelmann.

Dr. Gubelmann had been head of the Newport dye business when Du Pont purchased it in 1931 and he had come along with the business. Gubelmann was already a wealthy man, from his share of the purchase price, and he continued to become wealthier as the price of Du Pont stock continued to rise and as he continued to rise higher in the Company he had joined. He ended his career as director of manufacture for the organic chemicals department but in 1942 he was manager of the dyestuffs division. This rank gave him a free hand in matters of dye manufacture and research and he exercised that free hand freely, particularly in research.

Gubelmann took such an active part in research that many people thought he was director of research but he was not. That position, during the 1940s, was held by Dr. Harold W. Elley, the same man who had come to the dye works in 1917 to help in those first attempts to make sulfur black. So Elley was a veteran in the field of dyes but did not consider himself to be an expert, at least not as much of an expert as Gubelmann. Most people in Du Pont's dye business—Gubelmann in particular—concurred in this opinion and so at dye research reviews Gubelmann's was the dominant voice nearly all the time. Elley had interests that ranged in the broader fields but Gubelmann's interests were centered almost exclusively in dyes and his dominant personality gave dyes a dominant position at Jackson Laboratory.

Behind his back Gubelmann was called "Ivan, the Terrible" and that name reflected more than just some knowledge of Russian history on the part of those who used it. Dr. Gubelmann was a soft-spoken little man, only an inch or two taller than five feet, but when he came up with a research idea, which was often, he held onto it as tenaciously as a bulldog and he shook it vigorously and frequently like a terrier with a rat in its mouth. Consequently, to many down the line the term "Ivan, the Terrible" seemed to be a fair description of him.

He pursued many of his ideas to the point of technical and financial success but others were failures, as is always true for those who steer courses through the uncharted waters of research. One of his infrequent failures, which he was never able to get tried out in the plant, was a steam heated nutsch. A nutsch is a vacuum-operated filtering device for removing water or other solvents from solid materials. Gubelmann was convinced these devices would be more useful if a way could be found to keep the slurry of liquid and suspended solids warm while the filtration was proceeding. The dye works had many of these devices but they were all unheated, so Gubelmann had Jackson Laboratory make some small heated nutsches. All of them worked well, at least in Gubelmann's opinion, but the engineering department, which was outside his control, could never be persuaded to develop the design for a plant-size heated nutsch. Gubelmann shook this rat for several years before finally giving up on it.

While he never succeeded in obtaining the heated nutsch he longed for, Gubelmann did succeed in appointing many of the men who came along with him from Newport to high positions at Jackson Laboratory. One of these was John Tinker who was assistant director in 1942 and later on director. With the possible exception of Gubelmann himself, Tinker was probably the most capable chemist who came to Du Pont from Newport. In some respects he was definitely more capable than even "Ivan, the Terrible." When it came to analyzing a complex chemical problem and then putting it into simple language that others could easily understand he was without an equal in Jackson Laboratory. The director in 1942, William S. Calcott, was an erudite man who had done a lot of the work on TEL and neoprene but he lacked Tinker's expertise in dyes and he lacked Tinker's gift for simplicity and clarity in explaining a dye program. If Tinker had shared Gubelmann's enthusiasm for that heated nutsch it probably would have been built, but he never gave it more than the mild support which subordinates usually give to any pet idea of the boss.

Another Newport chemist promoted by "Ivan, the Terrible" was Dr. Otto Stallmann, head of the miscellaneous dyes division of Jackson Laboratory and originator of the "Stallmann number" for measuring the solubility of anthraquinone dyes.

It is difficult to conceive of a man who was less like what his background might be expected to produce than Otto Stallmann. He had been a German machine gunner during World War I, had survived the savage battles around Verdun and had a scarred left hand as a souvenir of those terrible days. He also had two gold filled teeth and sported a silver cigarette holder with a plunger to eject the stub after the cigarette had been smoked down to a residue of a few millimeters. However, at this point all resemblance to a proud Prussian warrior ceased.

Stallmann was a gentle, kindly man completely lacking in arrogance, guile, or malice and he was equipped with a fine sense of humor. His father had been a Lutheran minister in Germany, as were three of his brothers, and Stallmann himself was a devout Christian who gave ten percent of his gross income to the Lutheran church. In addition he made many other contributions to charity—particularly CARE packages when that program of foreign aid started after the war.

There were three dye divisions in Jackson Laboratory during the early 1940s and each division head was convinced that his was the most important. The azo dye division head

John M. Tinker was director of Jackson Laboratory during the 1950s when it was widely recognized as one of the great centers for research in organic chemistry. Tinker was one of the group of distinguished dye chemists who came to the Du Pont Company when it purchased the dye business of the Newport Company. Included in the group were Ivan ("The Terrible") Gubelmann and Otto Stallmann, the gentle German machine gunner.

pointed out that azo dyes accounted for more sales than any other group and the anthraquinone dye head said that while this was ture, the vat dyes were the highest quality dyes and in time would outgrow the azo. Both division heads pointed out that Stallmann's miscellaneous dyes division was concerned with the older dyes such as crystal violet and other triaryl methane colors that would be obsolete in a decade or so. However, Gubelmann and Tinker had assigned the research on the new "Monastral" colors to Stallmann's division, and these pigments represented the most important new development in the field of synthetic colors in thirty years. Also, Stallmann received more than his proportionate share of new chemists for their early training, and he smiled, but never retaliated, when these young chemists told him that the other dye groups believed his product line was headed for early obsolescence.

Stallmann signed all the memoranda that he sent to his organization with the first letter of his given name and the first two letters of his last name: O.St. So to the chemists who worked for him he was known as "Ost."

Ost regularly invited the young chemists in his division to have lunch with him at the river cafeteria close to Jackson Laboratory, and during these lunch sessions he taught them both dye chemistry and philosophy.

The war was constant agony for him in those days. He was a naturalized citizen of the United States and a loyal one, but all of his father's family and all of the friends of his youth were still living in Germany so that he was torn between powerful conflicting forces. There was real anguish in his voice when he spoke of what the Nazis had done to the Jews and equal anguish when he spoke of the suffering which he knew the Germans had endured in World War I and which he feared would soon be repeated.

Ost seldom had much to say about the bitter trench warfare he had struggled through himself and usually just shook his head when someone brought up the subject of World War I, but he spoke eloquently of the suffering his relatives

had endured during that war and during the incredible inflation which followed it.

"The winter of 1918 was the worst for Germany in that
war," he said. "I was at the front and usually had enough to
eat but my mother told me of the awful weeks when they
had nothing to eat except turnips. They had boiled turnips,
fried turnips, turnip soup, and even turnip bread until it got
so that the sight of turnips made them all sick."

Ost's aunt was a victim of the wild inflation of 1923
that wiped out the life savings of so many middle-class Germans.

"She was a widow with a small pension income," he
said, "and a good middle-class house which she thought for
many years was worth about fifteen thousand marks. The
inflation of 1922 had greatly reduced the value of her pension and she couldn't live on it so she slowly sold off most of
her personal belongings until she had only her house left.
One day a real estate broker offered her fifty thousand marks
for her house but she resisted because she knew she would
have no place to live if she sold it. Then a week or so later
in September of 1923 another broker offered her two hundred
thousand marks but she still resisted. Shortly after that she
was offered a million marks and it was too much for her. Her
daily needs were for huge numbers of marks and in addition
she had dreams of living like a millionaire. So she sold her
house and a week after she turned over the deed to it, her
million marks would not buy a loaf of bread or even a single
slice of bread. The old woman had nothing to eat and no place
to live."

Ost did not like to talk about his days as a university
student after the war but did occasionally tell how the professors were about as dictatorial as the army officers had
been. Ost was grateful, however, to one of these professors
who helped him make contact with Dr. Gubelmann at the
Newport Company in America when he came to this country
as a penniless young chemist.

"I was deeply grateful to Dr. Gubelmann for giving me

a job," he said, "until I got promoted and learned that he had started me at a salary about 30 percent less than he paid starting American chemists. Then I stopped being grateful for a while until he promoted me again and raised my salary far above all those who had started with me. I learned from that firsthand experience that generosity is a personal thing, and the man I think is a skinflint may be a hero to someone else, or vice versa. Actually, all Dr. Gubelmann was doing was paying what the market place demanded and I've learned that in business you have to do that or you get into trouble. However, I've never stopped being grateful to this country for giving me an opportunity to live and work here. Those who speak of its deficiencies and say they want a revolution of some sort never saw the kinds of things I saw in Germany when it was torn apart by war, revolution, and inflation."

One day during a lunch session one of Ost's bright young chemists, Dr. Stanley Krahler, who had been assigned to the "Monastral" color program, launched into a long theoretical discussion on the structure of the copper phthalocyanine (CPC) molecule that was basic to all the "Monastral" colors. He pointed out how statistically improbable it was that four phthalonitrile molecules would combine with one copper atom to form such a stable molecule as CPC.

"CPC would never form in the first place," Dr. Krahler continued "if it were not for the fact that the resonance energy in this complex molecule prevents it from flying apart, and that amazing amount of resonance is, of course, what causes it to be colored."

Dr. Krahler continued along that line for sometime, but when he finished Ost turned to him and said: "Do you suppose we will still be able to make CPC"?

This question broke up the lunch meeting but it was delivered in such a manner that Dr. Krahler knew Ost was laughing with him and not at him.

Perhaps the best illustration of how considerate Ost was of the feelings of others came on the occasion of A. J. Johnson's 25th anniversary with Du Pont.

There were three chemists named Johnson working for Ost at the time. One was A. J. Johnson, another was O. H. Johnson and the third was K. C. Johnson. These three were usually called by their initials. K. C. Johnson's initials were pronounced as "Casey" and he even signed his name that way at times. O. H. Johnson was sometimes called Hydroxy Johnson because the hydroxy group in chemistry consists of an oxygen atom (O) and a hydrogen atom (H).

A. J. Johnson was sometimes called "Silent" Johnson behind his back because he spoke very frugally, but Ost always called him "A.J." Anyway, on A.J.'s 25th anniversary the miscellaneous dyes division took him to lunch at the river cafeteria and Ost presented him with a 25 year pin and praised him for his long and distinguished service to the Du Pont Company. A.J. seemed to be in good health and spirits at the lunch but next day he did not report for work, and at lunch that day Ost told the story of what had happened.

"At about 8:15," he said "the phone rang and a woman's voice said to me 'Arthur doesn't feel good today and will not be in to work.' That puzzled me and I said to her 'who will not be in to work?' 'Arthur,' she said. Then I told her she must have the wrong number because I didn't know anyone named Arthur.' So she hung up the phone, but in a little while Mr. Tinker's secretary came to see me and said that the wife of one of my chemists, Arthur J. Johnson, had called Mr. Tinker's office because she said her husband had been working for Du Pont for 25 years, and still no one, not even his boss, had ever heard of him. Then I knew what a terrific mistake I had made so I called Mrs. Johnson back and apologized. She said she understood and it was all right but it isn't. Tonight I must stop by A.J.'s house and apologize in person."

And he did. A.J. reported, with an unusual twinkle in his eye, that "The door bell rang and when my wife went to answer it there stood my boss with his hat in his hand, a worried look on his face, and a long explanation of how important a man I am and how stupid he was not to know that my first name was Arthur."

That was Otto Stallmann, the man who had been sorely tested on the field of battle and who was to be sorely tested again during the commercial development of Du Pont's last major venture in the field of dyes and pigments, the "Monastral" blues and greens.

THOSE HEAVENLY BLUES AND GREENS ^{8}

The "Monastral" colors—blues and greens—were the Du Pont Company's last major effort to expand its dye business into a new field. These "Monastral" colors provided a condensed version of the company's entire experience in the dye business. That is to say, this final chapter was much like the entire book but shorter; the "Monastral" colors went from red ink to good profitability and back to red ink again in about one-third the time it took the entire dye business to do the same thing.

The word "Monastral" is a trademark name derived from "mono," meaning one, and "astral" meaning starlike, or heavenly. So a "Monastral" blue was one heavenly blue. At least it was in the eyes of the sales division people who coined the name.

But there was a lot of truth in that extravagant sounding name because these "Monastral" blues, and the greens too, had a better combination of brightness, strength, and stability than any colored material found in nature or developed in the chemical laboratories of the world. Victoria Pure Blue BO, so proudly named after England's famous Queen, had the brightness and strength but fell far short of the "Monastral" blues in stability, while most other blues, natural or synthetic, could not match these amazing colors in even two of the properties most desired in dyes and pigments.

Artists and printers quickly recognized the remarkable qualities of these colors when they first became available in the late 1930s.

When an artist sets out to paint a masterpiece—something he hopes will last for centuries—he almost invariably chooses a "Monastral" blue or green when these shades are a part of his conception. All high quality printing, of the type that brighten up the magazines and posters of today, also use "Monastral" blues and greens because printers know that these colors will endure the ravages of sunlight, ozone, and other degrading influences of the environment.

Chemically, both the "Monastral" blues and greens are derivations of the phthalocyanine molecule. With a few exceptions, these molecules are all derived from copper phthalocyanine but fortunately this long name has been shortened by the industry to three letters—CPC.

The similarity between the history of the "Monastral" colors (CPC) and earlier dyes starts right with the beginning. CPC was discovered by accident, just like Perkin's marvelous mauve was. Two chemists named de Diesbach and Van der Weid accidentally made CPC when they heated up copper cyanide with dibromobenzene and pyridine.

They saw that they had produced a blue material but they had no idea what it was or how it might be used, so they took no action toward making it into a commercial dye or pigment. And neither did anyone else for about six years.

However, de Diesbach did do one thing that later became important in determining what could be patented about CPC. He wrote a description of what he and his partner had done and published it in a Swiss chemical journal called *Helvetica Chimca Acta*. This article showed that he had not the foggiest notion about the true chemical structure of his new blue substance, or any realization that he had discovered a very valuable new material. But his publication did show beyond all reasonable doubt that de Diesbach had invented CPC, and this fact kept all others from being able, later, to get a product patent on CPC.

So CPC sat idle, so to speak, for six years until it was

rediscovered by some chemists working for the Scottish Dyes Corporation in England during the mid 1930s. These chemists accidentally made iron phthalocyanine, which was also blue although not nearly as bright and strong as copper phthalocyanine. Nevertheless, it intrigued them and they made a whole series of metal phthalocyanines. Included in this list was copper phthalocyanine—CPC—the magic blue which de Diesbach had looked at earlier.

A university professor named R. T. Linstead, then serving as a consultant for Scottish Dyes, was the man who did the most to show what an amazing molecule CPC was and how it might be used as a colored pigment. Linstead was the real pioneer for CPC even though he could not get a basic patent because of de Diesbach's published article. However, he did obtain a whole host of peripheral patents which were useful to him and his company.

As Dr. Stanley Krahler was to explain some years later to his boss, Dr. Otto Stallmann, the Jackson Laboratory machine gunner, CPC was as remarkable chemically as it was visually. The closest things to it in nature were the chlorophyl of green grass and red haemoglobin of blood. These molecules of nature were chelates just as CPC was but they lacked the amazing stability of CPC.

The CPC molecule, which Professor Linstead identified and of which he showed the chemical structure, was a most complex molecule indeed. It had four of Kekule's famous benzene rings symmetrically arranged around a larger ring with eight other rings inside, and at the center of it all was a copper atom. As Dr. Krahler said, it is likely that a team of the finest synthetic chemists in the world would have taken many years to figure out how to make it if Professor Linstead had shown them the structural formula for it but nothing else.

However, its two accidental discoveries suggested that if given a chance its components would more or less come together naturally, and during the 1930s and 1940s this was shown to be the case. CPC can be made easily by several routes and using a variety of starting materials. The simplest procedure involved heating two chemicals, copper chloride and phthalonitrile, together in a test tube. This was the aspect of CPC that so amazed Dr. Krahler; there was no need for an elaborate system of fitting the parts together as is usually true in synthetic organic chemistry. They all fall in place automatically, and it seems that the rings within rings were all a part of some grand scheme, like the solar system. So the name "Monastral" was not so preposterous after all to chemists. CPC was truly an astral molecule.

While the publication by de Diesbach in 1927 caused no stir at all and nothing happened for six years, Professor Linstead's disclosures in 1934 created a sensation and led to a frenzy of activity in the field of dyes and pigments. English, German, and American dye chemists dived into the field in a way that suggested they believed CPC might well be the most important development in colored materials in a quarter of a century.

And future events proved they were right. CPC was not only the most important new discovery in dyes and pigments for over twenty-five years but was the last major development in the field during the twentieth century. Nearly half a century has gone by since Linstead published his first paper on CPC and nothing of comparable importance in dyes and pigments has occurred in all that time.

Hundreds of new individual dyes have been invented and thousands of improvements in old dyes have been made, but all of these advances combined have not equalled that flash of light and color that accompanied the advent of those heavenly blues and greens, the "Monastral" colors, or CPC.

The CPC colors were so exciting that Du Pont began to study them in two different industrial departments—the pigments department of Newark, N.J. and the organic chemicals department's Jackson Laboratory at the dye works.

This duplication of research work at Du Pont occurred for several reasons, one of which was that Americans have always been hung up on a definition for the word "dye." The general public thinks of it as any colored substance, but chemists tend to be more restrictive and say that a dye is a soluble colored material which can be used to color cloth or paper. An insoluble colored material that can be used to make paints or inks is a pigment, they say. The various definitions are often more technical and complicated than the above but the basic idea is always the same: a dye is soluble and colors fibers while a pigment is insoluble and colors paints or inks.

However, even the most sophisticated definitions tend to flounder around in the complex techniques for using dyes and pigments that have grown up in the past hundred years. For example, the anthraquinone colors are recognized by all as dyes but they really are pigments. That is to say, they are not soluble in water but are suspended solids which are solublized by chemical treatment either before or after they are applied to the fiber being dyed. Other pigments are never solublized at all but are nevertheless used to color cloth using a binder of some sort to hold the pigment on the cloth.

The Germans avoided much of the confusion about what is a dye and what is a pigment by lumping them both into one group which they called "farbestoffe" which can be translated into "colored stuff." The giant German dye company, I. G. Farbenindustrie, did the same sort of combining with its name since "Farbenindustrie" can be translated into "color industry" thereby including both dyes and pigments.

The Du Pont Company was further ripe for confusion as to where CPC should be made ready for commercialization because CPC was an organic chemical and therefore the organic chemicals department thought it was included in their charter. But CPC was also a pigment so the pigments department thought it clearly belonged to them.

The question was one that normally would have been decided by the executive committee of the board of directors, but it was not—for two reasons: first, when the duplication of research began in the middle 1930s no one was sure that CPC really would become commercially important even though two departments thought it would, and the company's top executives did not wish to stifle any good ideas, regardless of where they sprang up. Second, the whole development occurred so swiftly that both departments had, by 1940, found markets which the other could not sell easily, if at all.

In any event, the research work on CPC proceeded quite independently in two locations and both departments were later authorized to build commercial plants to manufacture "Monastral" colors for their special markets. The pigments department would sell pigment to ink and paint manufacturers while the organic chemicals department would sell pastes, water dispersible powders, press cakes, and dry powders to its customers some of which overlapped those of the pigments department.

It is a long established and fundamental law of chemistry that "if it was not invented here then it is no good," so while the two departments had access to the research work of each other, it is not surprising that they came up with different processes, Not only were the processes for the crude blue and green pigments different but so were the finishing steps. That is to say, the procedures for reducing the particle size of the crude pigments to a strong, bright finished color were quite different.

The pigments department milled their crude pigments with shot in a mill partly filled with acetone while the organic chemicals department either milled with pebbles and salt or dissolved the crude pigment in strong sulfuric acid and ran this solution into vigorously agitated water, causing the pigment to be precipitated from solution in very fine particles. In making the green pigment one department chlorinated the blue pigment in a solution of sulfur chloride while the other used aluminum chloride.

Not surprisingly, the finished pigments had different physical properties even though they were chemically quite similar. The phthalocyanine blues and greens made at Newport were "softer" and more stable in the ink or paint vehicles, while those at Chambers Works were "jetter" but often quite unstable in the inks and paints made from them.

These differences in properties led to great confusion in the marketplace, with some customers contending that Du Pont was holding back its best pigments for internal use in its own F. & F. department, or selling its best products to favored customers of either the pigments department or the organic chemicals department. There was no truth to these charges because both departments were trying desperately to please all customers, but customers who received "soft," stable powders wanted "jetter" products and those who received the jetter products wanted soft stable ones—they felt there was no reason why they couldn't have the desirable properties from both processes.

But the production supervisors, at Chambers Works in particular, were having great trouble in reproducing the products which came naturally from their own processes, much less combining the best qualities of both processes. All the start-up problems, which had plagued the early efforts to produce dyes at Chambers Works in 1917, came back to haunt the CPC plant despite the fact that the top young chemical engineer at Chambers Works, Bob Stevens, had been brought over from Ed Fielding's division to head up "Monastral" colors. And Stevens had been supplemented by Denny Compton and Al Bilancioni who had learned about CPC from their work in the small-scale plant that had operated near Jackson Laboratory for almost a decade.

In addition to all the start-up problems at Chambers Works, the organic chemicals department had another serious problem; due to the nature of the markets it serviced, most of the "Monastral" blues and greens from the Chambers Works sold at a price that was 15% lower than the price obtained by the pigments department.

The different processes, different quality standards, and different prices of the two different departments soon led to vast confusion on "Monastral" colors within the Du Pont

Company, and the old principle of "if it was not invented here then it is no good" rose to heights seldom reached before.

Some people in the pigments department claimed that those at Chambers Works knew little or nothing about the manufacture of pigments and that, in addition, the organic chemicals department was selling, at a 15% discount, markets which they could sell at a full price. They concluded that the Chambers Works plant for CPC should be shut down and the entire "Monastral" colors business be turned over to the pigments department.

On the other hand, some people in the organic chemicals department argued that their processes were inherently superior to those in their sister department and that this would become evident as soon as start-up problems were solved. Furthermore, they said, the pigments department had no processes at all for making such things as printing pastes for coloring textile fibers, soluble dyes, and water dispersible powders to color paper.

While this intramural competition was bubbling along merrily in its early stages the organic chemicals department was usually on the defensive because the pigments department's new "Monastral" plant reached a state of profitability much earlier than did the plant at Chambers Works. Some of the "Monastral" colors made at Chambers Works, such as the blue and green pastes sold to textile printing houses, and to the 3M company for use in coloring roofing granules, quickly became profitable, mostly because they were sold without the 15% discount. The blue and green powders and press cakes, which made up the bulk of the business, either stayed in the red or were at best borderline in profitability. So doubts began to develop, even at Chambers Works, whether these products would ever become profitable.

In the midst of all this doubt the general manager of the organic chemicals department, E. G. Robinson, retired and he was replaced by John F. ("Jack") Daley who had been general manager of the rival pigments department! This appointment made by the executive committee was promptly declared by some people in the organic chemicals department to be a Machiavellian move designed to bring about the prompt death of "Monastral" colors at Chambers Works. This was because it was assumed that Jack Daley had surely been thoroughly indoctrinated by his former associates with the concept that the organic chemicals department knew next to nothing about manufacturing pigments and should turn the business over to those who understood it.

If Daley had any such notions he never disclosed them, and he was soon deluged with an avalanche of contrary propaganda launched at him by his new department. And while he was digesting this information, the "Monastral" color business at Chambers Works began to improve. Some of the products derived from CPC, such as "Luxol" Fast Blue MBS used in ball-point pen inks, and "Pontamine" Fast Turquoise 8GL used in dyeing cotton, even developed higher margins of profit than any of the "Monastral" blues and greens being sold by the pigments department.

These facts, along with optimistic forecasts on a variety of dyes that the research division said would be developed from CPC, but for which the pigments department had no plans, carried the day and "Monastral" colors were allowed to run their course at Chambers Works. This course was an erratic one but its trend was upward and for a decade or so "Monastral" colors at Chambers Works were reasonably profitable, particularly during periods of high business activity.

Then as already noted, these heavenly blues and greens began a decline in profitability which preceded the decline of dyes in general. High wages, high overhead costs, and strong domestic and foreign competition from firms with lower wages and lower overhead costs were the principal causes for the decline in profitability, just as they were at a later date for dyes in general.

But before the sad day of reckoning arrived, one of the new dyes derived from CPC and promised to Jack Daley by

John F. ("Jack") Daley was general manager of the organic chemicals department during one period of high prosperity for dyes. Daley had the full approval of personnel manager Claude Thompson, although the U.S. Surgeon-General might have held back part of his. (Photography by Karsh, Ottawa.)

the research division, went through an even briefer rise and fall than "Monastral" colors in general followed. The new dye was "Sulfogene" Brilliant Green J, a cotton dye which Dr. Herbert Lubs told Daley would become another "Ponsol" Jade Green. This was high praise indeed because Jade Green was, at that time, the greatest success story that Du Pont's dye business had ever known.

WYETH AND LUBS 9

Dr. Herbert A. Lubs, the man who encouraged Jack Daley to believe that "Sulfogene" Brilliant Green J would earn millions of dollars for the Du Pont Company, was a remarkable man.

In fact, Lubs was in some ways the most remarkable of all the brilliant band of chemists who caused dyes to be one of Du Pont's shining lights of profitability for over two decades. His restless, darting eyes, reflecting an equally restless and inquisitive mind, were dark like his complexion, and consisted mostly of pupils which were so large and round that they often caused people who met him for the first time to think of Little Orphan Annie and the large circles which served her as eyes.

Lubs certainly was the most enthusiastic and eternally optimistic of all the chemists who worked on dye research during the days of glory for dyes when Jack Daley and Sam Baker were general managers of the organic chemicals department. To Lubs the impossible dream simply did not exist in the field of dyes; if it could be imagined it could be done. And like that other great dreamer of dreams, Cervantes' man of La Mancha, when Lubs set out in pursuit of his goals he was always willing to fight the unbeatable foe or reach for the unreachable stars.

His enthusiasm for dyes kept him in a state of both

Dr. Herbert A. Lubs was assistant director of research and in that capacity managed many dye success stories. Green J was another story.

mental and physical motion. His head twisted from side to side and his chin jerked up and down, like a man wearing a shirt collar a size too small, and he squirmed in his seat whenever he discussed dye research.

During most of the glory days for Du Pont dyes, Lubs served as assistant director of research under his long-time friend, Dr. Harold Elley, the man who helped start up the sulfur black plant in 1917, and the two of them decided to retire at the same time. Their associates held a retirement party in honor of this distinguished pair of chemists and friends and associates from all over the country came to pay tribute to them.

When it came Lubs's time to speak that night he startled the audience by declaring: "My friends, I have found serenity." But even as he spoke those words it was obvious that they represented a hope and not a reality because he was twisting his head and bobbing his chin in the fashion that had long been characteristic of him. Further evidence that Lubs and serenity had not settled down together came when he later became a consultant for the Maumee Chemical company.

"During the first year of his consulting job," a Maumee vice-president said, "Herb fed us enough ideas to keep our research division occupied for a hundred years."

Lubs' enthusiasm for dyes was infectious and caused dozens of his associates and subordinates to join him in reaching for the unreachable stars. They missed some, of course, but they grabbed enough to keep the dye business bright and glittering for thirty to forty years.

One star that Lubs and his associates reached for was the aforementioned "Sulfogene" Brilliant Green J, hereafter to be known simply as Green J.

Green J was a dye in the same sense that the anthraquinone and sulfur colors were dyes. That is, it could be dissolved in water and sodium hydroxide, adsorbed onto cotton fibers and then oxidized to produce the dyed cloth, in typical "vat" dye fashion. The concept of making a vat dye based on

CPC was one of the organic chemicals department's arguments when it insisted that all CPC work should not be turned over to the pigments department. True, CPC was a pigment; but a soluble dye derived from this magnificent basic molecule was not, and so the pigments department should not have exclusive rights to all CPC developments.

The logic to this argument was irrefutable and following it Lubs and his associates had already scored two minor successes: "Pontamine" Fast Turquoise 8GL and "Luxol" Fast Blue MBS. The Turquoise was a true cotton dye which was highly profitable but did not sell in large quantities. The Blue was probably the best dye for ball point inks ever invented and it had a profit margin which exceeded the best of the pigments department's CPC products. But the "Luxol" Blue was even smaller in sales volume than the Turquoise because a pound of it would make enough ink for thousands of pens.

Lubs and his associates contended that Green J would be different. It would not only be an artistic triumph but also a huge financial success, because it would sell even more pounds than the fabulous anthraquinone Jade Green which had already made millions for Du Pont.

The proposed process devised by Lubs and his associates for making Green J from the basic CPC molecule was simple enough in outline form: 1) First make Tetra nitro CPC, 2) Reduce this to Tetra amino CPC, 3) Diazontize all four amino groups, and 4) Replace the diazo groups with mercapto groups to make Tetra Mercapto CPC. This was Green J.

While the process outlined above requires only three or four printed lines to describe it, a group of six chemists spent a total of about four man-years in working out the details. But the end result seemed to be worth the trouble. Green J was a bright yellow shade of green which many people in both the research and sales divisions thought would be more attractive to the public than the fabulous Jade Green had been. It was at this point that Lubs explained to Daley what a gold mine the research division had come up with. It was all very convincing, and so the money required to install manufacturing facilities for Green J in the "Monastral" plant was authorized at once and the facilities were quickly purchased and put in place.

Then the age old problem of plant start-up, which has existed for dyes since Perkin made his first batch of mauve in 1857, reappeared. The process that worked so beautifully in the laboratory ran into all sorts of problems when it was scaled up a thousand fold in the plant. It was like 1917 all over again for Du Pont.

The first two attempts to make a thousand pounds of Green J yielded only about two hundred pounds and it was so much bluer and duller than the standard already set up and sampled to the textile industry, that the sales division refused to offer it to their customers at any price. Subsequent productions came closer in shade to the standard and finally the sales division reluctantly agreed to ship some of it to the industry, but they had little enthusiasm for Green J because the cost of manufacturing a pound of it was three or four times as great as the selling price.

This situation continued for five or six months and, as in the past, differences of opinion between the research and manufacturing divisions grew up as to why this was so. The manufacturing people said the process was inherently a poor one and obviously could not be operated on a plant scale, but the research division said the trouble lay in the fact that the manufacturing people were an ignorant bunch of barrel rollers who could not be trusted to operate any process, no matter how foolproof it was. There may have been some truth to all these charges and counter charges but the process did however consistently produce standard quality Green J in the laboratory. When the research chemists went out in the plant to watch the ignorant barrel rollers and find out what they were doing wrong the Green J still came out blue and dull and in low yield.

Jack Daley had seen start-up problems many times

before, in his old department when they first tried to make CPC and in other places, so he was reasonably patient with the failures on Green J, although he could not resist the temptation to ask Lubs, from time to time, what had happened to those millions of dollars that Green J was supposed to earn for Du Pont. Finally, however, his patience wore out and he urged Lubs to admit that the whole thing had been a mistake and that work on Green J should be stopped. Whereupon Daley, formidable manager of men though he was, learned something that others in the organic chemicals department had known for a long time: no one was able to cause Lubs to say something he did not wish to say or do something he did not wish to do. Daley's assistant general manager at the time, Sam Lenher, another formidable manager of men, had the same experience with Lubs so the general management of the department put Green J on the back burner and forgot about it.

But Lubs did not. He decided that the manufacturing people responsible for Green J would do better if they were given some gentle stroking rather than continued doses of criticism. So he instructed Dr. Stanley Dietrick, who was in charge of Green J at Jackson Laboratory, to bring the chief supervisor in charge of Green J in the plant to Wilmington for lunch at the Brandywine Room in the Hotel du Pont.

The Brandywine Room has been famous in Wilmington for over half a century for its good food, but is even more famous for the fact that it has one of the finest collections of Wyeth original paintings in the world displayed on its walls. There are six paintings by Andrew Wyeth, two by his son, Jamie Wyeth, two by his nephew, A. N. Wyeth, and one by his father, N. C. Wyeth. These paintings, at current market prices, are valued at well over a million dollars, but the Hotel had purchased all but the one by N. C. Wyeth, when the artists were young and relatively unknown. Now it is generally accepted as a fact around Wilmington that all Wyeths are geniuses, and Andrew Wyeth is so regarded all over the world. Consequently, the Brandywine Room's collection of

Wyeth art is treasure of great value, with Andrew's paintings being generally regarded as the most valuable.

Nevertheless, it is the one painting by N. C. Wyeth, the man who started the dynasty of Wyeth artists, that dominates the scene in the Brandywine Room.

Most of the Wyeth paintings are done with subdued colors but this one by N. C. Wyeth, called *The Island Funeral*, offers a magnificent display of colors, mostly brilliant blues and greens, and has been given the most prominent position of them all, right above the mantelpiece at the south end of the room. It shows a small flotilla of boats assembling around a tiny island off the coast of Maine. The time of the year appears to be fall because the grass around the house at the center of the island is done in the more typical Wyeth colors of brown and tan, but what catches the eye of all observers is the breathtaking beauty of the blues and greens in the water around the island. And as is so often the case with paintings by all the Wyeths, this picture evokes a flood of thoughts and memories that almost overwhelm the viewer. It would be foolish for anyone to try to describe how *The Island Funeral* creates this sensation, but it does; it is the work of a genius and genius defies explanation.

Dr. Lubs had reserved a table right below *The Island Funeral* and as soon as he and his guests were seated he began to talk about it.

"Boys," he said to his visitors from across the river "take a look at this magnificent painting because it illustrates how much science and industry are a part of art. It is almost impossible to say where science ends and art begins. This masterpiece from the hand of one of the greatest of all American artists could not have been painted a few years ago because some of the pigments in it did not exist then. Those blues and greens are "Monastral" colors made in the semi-works at Jackson Laboratory. The blue is copper phthalocyanine and the green is polychloro copper phthalocyanine. I personally gave them to N. C. Wyeth and told him how to blend them into his painting oils. There has never been anything like them in the world before and they will be just as beautiful a hundred years in the future as they are right now. Just think what Titian and Rembrandt might have done if they had been able to obtain blues and greens of the quality which N. C. Wyeth used here."

Lubs continued on at length telling how the blue and green pigments that he gave N. C. Wyeth had been prepared as crudes and then finished to soft powders which an artist could rather easily incorporate into his oils. He handed out so many compliments to the painting, dividing them so nearly in equal parts between the artist and the pigments he had used, that Dietrick, who knew him well, finally interrupted his monologue.

"Herb," Dietrick said, "maybe you should sign the picture too. Make it Wyeth and Lubs or maybe Lubs and Wyeth."

"Yes," Dr. Lubs replied. But then he moved on so swiftly to further details about the quality of the pigments that his listeners were not sure whether he was saying yes to Wyeth and Lubs, to Lubs and Wyeth, or just to the idea in general.

Anyway, the lunch was nearly over before he got around to the topic of Green J. Then he pointed out again how closely art and science are related.

"Remember, boys," he said, "when you finally get Green J straightened out you will be doing more than just making money for the Du Pont Company. You will be adding beauty to the world because the textile industry has never before had available to it such a bright, stable shade of green for dyeing cotton."

Then amazingly in a few months the production supervisors at Chambers Works did solve their scale-up problems and began to make Green J in good yields and high quality. The sales division sold most of this new production promptly and it began to seem that Green J might indeed make millions for Du Pont because when it was made properly the mill cost was only a small fraction of the selling price.

Then the fickle public, which already had a dozen or so dyes available for every shade in the rainbow, lost interest

On the occasion of his retirement, Dr. Lubs was congratulated by William C. ("Bill") Kay who succeeded Sam Baker as general manager of the organic chemicals department. Bill Kay kept his eyes open when he was at work, but seemed to be having trouble here.

in Green J and sales fell almost to zero. Like the old soldier in General MacArthur's song, it just faded away.

Shortly thereafter Jack Daley was promoted and made a Du Pont vice-president, a position to which his assistant, Sam Lenher, had already gone. In fact, the organic chemicals department began to develop a reputation as a breeder of vice-presidents because George Holbrook, who had served in both Jackson Laboratory and the Chambers Works, also became a vice-president. It would be absurd to suggest that the careers of these three men had been aided by Green J which had a period of profitability lasting only a few months. But

Dr. George E. Holbrook started his career with Du Pont as a chemist and softball player at Jackson Laboratory. He later became assistant general manager of the organic chemicals department and was the first general manager of the new elastomer chemicals department. Still later, he became an executive vice-president of Du Pont. He was one of three executive vice-presidents whose careers were not aided by the brightest of all green sulfur colors, "Sulfogene" Brilliant Green J. This dye was developed by Jackson Laboratory during a period of five years, but it was profitable for only six months. (Photograph courtesy of the Public Affairs Department, E. I. du Pont de Nemours & Company.)

all three of them realized that Green J was not the first, and probably would not be the last time that a research division offered a pot of gold to a vice-president, only to have both the pot and the rainbow above it disappear when he reached out to pull it in.

DARLING OF THE DYE WORKS

10

The Basic Colors Area of the dye works and the man who managed it, Joshua Ferris Darling, were both highly regarded by the chemists of Jackson Laboratory during the 1940s when dyes were in one of their periods of high profitability. And there were good reasons why this was so.

Whenever Jackson Laboratory developed a new dye the chemists involved were eager to have it make as much money as possible. This concern by the chemists about profits was only obliquely related to the interests of Du Pont's stockholders, but was directly related to the interests of the chemists themselves. If the new dye made a lot of money the chemists could expect substantial bonuses immediately, followed by promotions as time went by, so their interest in profits was genuine and persistent. Furthermore, all of the chemists knew that if their new dye was turned over to Darling and his Basic Colors Area for manufacture then it had a better than average chance of becoming highly profitable.

Unfortunately, so far as the chemists were concerned, in most cases they had no control over where a new dye would be manufactured. A new azo dye was almost certain to be assigned to the Azo Colors Area, a new vat dye to the "Ponsol" Colors Area, and other products to other designated areas that already had the equipment required to manufacture them. In this way the investment in the six areas devoted to dye manufacture could be kept as low as possible and the return on investment as high as possible.

However, some new dyes did not clearly belong to any existing area of dye manufacture and so were, in a sense, up for grabs. The "Monastral" blues and greens were an example of this free agent type of new dye that, in theory at least, might be assigned to any one of six manufacturing areas at the Chambers Works. Actually, there was never much of a contest for "Monastral" colors. They became a part of the Basic Colors Area because of the low fixed costs that existed there, and because Darling had a long-established reputation for quickly making new products profitable and then keeping them that way.

Part of this reputation had been inherited from his predecessor, Dr. Edmund C. Humphrey, who had been a master in keeping fixed costs low, but most of it had been earned by Darling himself because of his extraordinary abilities as a leader and manager. He seemed to have an instinctive feeling for what made sense technically, and his performance in employee relations was outstanding. All of his associates, peers, subordinates, and superiors trusted both his honesty and his judgment. These two things were partly responsible for the fact that average costs in his area were lower than in most other locations in the plant. Another factor that contributed to low costs in Darling's area was related to plant age. The newer areas, such as Azo Colors and "Ponsol" Colors, tended to have higher fixed charges because the buildings and equipment had been installed more recently, were more expensive, and consequently had higher depreciation costs.

But there was more to the low costs found in the Basic Colors Area than just the age of the facilities. The manufacture of Sulfur Black in the Sulfur Colors Area and Auramine in the Basic Colors Area had both started at about the same time, but Sulfur Black had encountered all sorts of problems that lasted a year or two, while Auramine had started to make money at once and continued to do so for thirty years.

In fact, the profitability pattern started by Auramine had become characteristic of the entire Basic Colors Area.

This did not mean that the Basic Colors Area never had any failures. However, when they occurred a rather quick recovery usually followed. For example, eosine, the dye used to make red ink, had been profitable for a year or two when World War I cut off supplies from Germany, but then began to lose money. This was because eosine was relatively easy to manufacture and soon there were so many competitors in the field that the price fell to a point where no one was making much of a profit and Du Pont went out of the business. A similar fate had befallen Magenta and Victoria green that had been made in the Magenta and Victoria Green buildings. Competition drove the prices so low that only manufacturers with very low fixed costs could compete, and Du Pont abandoned these two dyes also.

The Basic Colors Area, however, had long before the 1940s established a reputation for quickly recovering from such failures. Dispersed rubber colors, which were more profitable than eosine had ever been, were being manufactured in the Eosine Building, and Victoria blues and Rhodamine reds, all highly profitable, had taken the place of magenta in the Magenta Building.

In addition to these specific items, the Basic Colors Area managers had fought overhead costs with remarkable persistence and success ever since Dr. Humphrey had been put in charge of the area. The Chambers Works had a clear definition of what overhead costs were, but, Humphrey regarded just about everything, except his own salary and the wages of his operators, as overhead and he fought a never-ending battle to reduce it. He was convinced that the Chambers Works engineering division, which was supposed to do all maintenance and repair work for the manufacturing areas, was too large and top-heavy to work efficiently, so he did all he could to by-pass these engineers. He had his foremen equip their operators with paint cans and brushes so the operators could do touch-up painting during spare moments, and he

Humphery
& Roberts, Inc.
FINE DYE MANUFACTURERS

Specializing in chromophores such as:
— sulfur colors
— azo colors
— anthraquinone
— triphenyl methanes
— phthalocyanines

"Crystal Violet Our Favorite"

MANUFACTURING DIVISION
Whitey Roberts

R&D
Dr. Edmund C. Humphrey

ADVERTISING
P.J. Wingate

TO DR. HUMPHREY:
WHEN YOU, WHITEY, AND PHIL LAUNCH YOUR NEW DYE BUSINESS
I'LL BE GLAD TO BE YOUR EMPLOYEE RELATIONS MANAGER.

P. Coleman du Pont 7-14-79

Inspired by a story in the Wilmington News-Journal Papers, T. Coleman du Pont prepared and presented this plaque to Dr. E. C. Humphrey shortly after Humphrey reached the age of 91. He gave a duplicate to Whitey Roberts who had recently celebrated the 95th anniversary of his birth. Young Coly was at that time the only direct descendant, with the last name of du Pont, still working for the Company founded by E. I. du Pont de Nemours.

personally brought shingles into the plant so that roof repairs could be done by the operators without paying any "overhead" charges from either the engineering or central stores organizations.

The engineering division contended that Humphrey's practices simply added to the overhead burden that other manufacturing areas had to bear, but this did not stop him. Humphrey said that if all areas followed his practices then the engineering division would be forced to become less top-heavy and everyone would benefit from the change.

This argument about overhead lasted throughout the history of dyes at Chambers Works and was never settled to the satisfaction of all. But in the meantime, Humphrey was repeatedly promoted and finally became a production manager with an office in Wilmington.

Humphrey was succeeded at the Basic Colors Area by the aforementioned Joshua Ferris Darling, called "J.F." by everyone who knew him. J.F. was forced to abandon many of Humphrey's practices of by-passing the engineering and other "overhead" organizations, but he continued the Humphrey habit of making the Basic Colors Area the lowest cost manufacturing unit in the plant. He also developed a whole host of cost reduction practices of his own which were more orthodox than Humphrey's, but just as effective.

J.F. was a tall, skinny man built along the lines of Connie Mack, the old Philadelphia baseball manager, whom he admired. Today he would be called "laid back" or "cool." That is to say, he was a successful man who knew he was successful and thus had no burning desire to advance higher in the organization. Or at least he never showed any, and always maintained very friendly relationships with the long series of subordinates who trained under him and later moved above him.

The part of Chambers Works which J.F. managed consisted of seven manufacturing units (the Auramine, Safranine, Eosine, Methyl violet, Victoria Green, Magenta, and Crystal Violet buildings), one laboratory and a change house, all of which were spread over about ten acres of land. His office was in the central administration building where he sat facing a rolltop desk into which he swept all unfinished business at the end of each day.

The contents of J.F.'s desk varied, of course, from day to day but two items were always present—a small calculus book and a copy of the King James Bible—both of which he studied during periods when business did not press him too heavily. And he usually managed to find such periods nearly every day.

The calculus book must have been used solely for recreation since there were no daily problems related to dye manufacture that required the application of either differential or integral calculus, but his interest in the Bible probably was a more complex affair.

J.F.'s behavior was always highly moral, but he never made any attempt to persuade others in the plant to accept his religious beliefs. If he read the Bible for divine guidance this was not obvious because he never quoted from it in an attempt to justify his beliefs or decisions. It was obvious that he took delight in the graceful English of the King James Bible and at times was wryly amused by some of the things he found there. Perhaps his attitude was similar to that of Bishop William Temple who advised his followers to "keep your wits about you while reading the Bible." At least this appeared to be the case when J.F. was helping to decide what should be done about a batch of Rhodamine B that became heavily contaminated with a blue dye.

The grinding and mixing area had put five thousand pounds of Rhodamine B into a blender that had previously been used to mix Victoria Blue, but no attempt had been made to sweep out the last traces of the blue dye so four or five pounds of the blue got mixed in with the red Rhodamine. This was enough contamination to cause the Rhodamine to be far too blue in shade to match its standard, so it was rejected by the sales division. The batch of Rhodamine had a sales value of about $30,000 so the problem was serious enough to justify a review by representatives of both the manufacturing and sales division.

In this review it was estimated that it would cost five or ten thousand dollars to rework the contaminated Rhodamine and even then the resulting product would be somewhat more blue in shade than it should be. At this point the sales division proposed that the contaminated Rhodamine B be sold, as is, in Du Pont's export markets.

J.F. objected to this at first, but finally agreed to the proposal when the sales division said the off-quality dye would be sold at a reduced price and under another name so that the reputation of Du Pont Rhodamine B would not be damaged.

However, he remained uncertain that the proper decision had been reached and when he came back from Wilmington he told his chief supervisor about his doubts.

"The whole thing," he said, "reminds me of the 21st verse in chapter 14 of the Book of Deuteronomy."

The chief supervisor said he was not familiar with this verse and J.F. then reached into his rolltop desk, pulled out his Bible, and read from it:

> *Ye shall not eat of anything that dieth of*
> *itself: thou shalt give it unto the stranger*
> *that is in thy gates that he may eat it; or*
> *thou mayest sell it unto an alien . . .*

J.F.'s eyes sparkled as he read this passage and the thin mustache on his upper lip was dancing when he added: "That kind of advice may be good for keeping down ptomaine poisoning among the hometown boys, but it sure is no way to build either a tourist or an export business."

In managing the Basic Colors Area J.F. had both a daily and a weekly routine. The daily routine included a walking tour of his seven manufacturing buildings and the laboratory. This tour was partly for employee relations and partly for finding out the state of production first hand, but mostly for safety purposes. J.F. had an eagle eye for anything which looked like an unsafe practice or poor house-keeping that could lead to an injury. He said very little during the course of the tours, other than to greet everyone by his first name. Operators, foremen, and supervisors all knew that he was there to offer help if it was needed, but woe to any supervisor who allowed an example of poor house-keeping to carry over from one inspection to the next. The offender could depend on it that he would be summoned to J.F.'s office for a conference that was always brief but always pointed.

The research and development work carried out in the area laboratory was a part of J.F.'s responsibility and his weekly routine included a laboratory conference during which the chemists reported on what they had done during the past week. J.F. operated with a loose rein on his chemists.

"They have to be allowed to make their own mistakes and occasionally reinvent the wheel," he said in explaining why he seldom gave direct orders on research. "And besides that, I suppose it is possible that I don't already know everything there is to be known about Basic Colors."

It is also possible that J.F. found these laboratory report sessions boring at times because he often listened to them with his eyes closed. No one knew whether he was sleeping during these closed eye periods because he also had a habit of asking questions with his eyes still closed. What made this technique particularly hard to diagnose was his practice of asking a question about some statement the speaker had made several sentences back. Sometimes when he gave a sudden jerk to his long outstretched legs the speaker might be convinced he had been napping, for on such occasions his subsequent questions were always directed at a topic further in the past than usual. These questions were always pertinent and usually incisive so, again, no one could be sure that he had not been awake all along.

When J.F. reached retirement age, Jim Reed, who once had been his chief supervisor before jumping over him to become general superintendent of all dye manufacture, told him that Chambers Works would suffer an irreplaceable loss in knowledge and wisdom when he retired. Reed said he had an understanding of the "know-how" of dye manufacture that no one else then had or was ever likely to develop in the future.

J.F. would have none of that. "It simply isn't so, Jim," he said. "People like Ford and Hess already know more about dyes in general than I do and they are still learning. Besides that you have young fellows like Stryker, Letang, and Hurka coming along, and if you need him enough you probably would be able to get Elton Cole back from the atomic energy program."

Shortly before he did retire, two of J.F.'s young supervisors decided to leave Du Pont and train for the ministry. When the second one made his intentions known, the chief supervisor of the Basic Colors Area went to J.F. and asked him if an attempt should be made to persuade the young man to change his mind.

"He is a good man, he knows his job now and we badly need experienced men," the chief supervisor said.

"No," J.F. replied. "Let him go. We have been losing men to the ministry, off and on, for twenty years so this is nothing new to me. I have a set speech which I give to any young man who tells me he wants to quit Du Pont and go to another industrial firm. I remind him that he is already working for what is probably the best company in the world, but that speech somehow loses something when the young man is going to work for the Lord. So just let him go and wish him good luck."

Then a twinkle came in his eye and he added: "But it does worry me at times because I wonder whether the way we behave inspires or frightens them into the ministry."

One day J.F. told Reed that he personally had lent $300 to an operator for a down payment on a house. "It may be the last of that $300 I'll ever see," he added.

Reed accused him of being a cynic, and J.F. replied: "Of course I'm a cynic. How can any man looking at human behavior, including my own, be anything except a cynic. But you don't have to be a mean one."

Despite the fact that he rather frequently made disparaging remarks about himself, J.F was by no means an insecure man. He had a solid confidence in his own judgment and this confidence continued long after he had retired from the Chambers Works. A decade or so after the war was over one of J.F.'s lieutenants from his Chambers Works days stopped by to visit him at his home in Woodstown, New Jersey. It was the day after an Army-Navy football game and J.F. was eager to talk football.

"The good football players just aren't going to the service academies any more," he said, "and that worries me. The quarterbacks in particular worry me. Yesterday Navy's quarterback seemed to be trying to give the game to Army, but the Army boy refused to take it. While I was watching that sad exhibition it occurred to me that some day the defenses of the nation might be in the hands of those two quarterbacks. It made me shudder for the national security."

J.F. was about seventy-five years old then, and surely had not played football for many years.

NO OTHER BOOK ¹¹

In some circles it is claimed that all businessmen are crooks and the bigger the business the bigger the crooks.

There probably is no truth to this claim regardless of where it is made, and it certainly was not true during the 1950s at Du Pont's Chambers Works, then the largest individual plant in the world's largest chemical company. The people at Chambers Works, from the plant manager on down to the messenger who carried mail around the plant were a remarkably moral group.

Frank Knowles, who was plant manager during this period of high profitability for dyes, was a philosophical man with a very high code of ethics and a sense of humor to give balance to his moral judgments. He was a member of the vestry of the Episcopal Church and on several occasions complained to the assistant plant manager about the way his fellow vestryman, Ned Railing, tried to persuade his associates to accept Railing's views as to how the church should be run.

"He usually says, 'The Lord wants us to do this or that'," Knowles reported, "but what I want to know is how does he know what the Lord wants us to do? I face the same problems Railing speaks of, but the Lord never says a word to me."

Frank Knowles was manager of the Chambers Works from 1948 to 1961. During that time he was forced to make wage increase decisions, he said, without the aid of divine guidance.

Knowles also had the same lament when he was negotiating a wage increase with the Union.

"The Union representatives come to me and claim that a wage increase, ranging from six cents an hour for helpers to nine cents for special operators, is just and morally right, while the five to eight cents which I am willing to agree to is immorally low. How does anyone know that five cents is immoral while six cents is just and right? I'd have trouble, on a moral basis, deciding between five and ten cents. It really is a matter of trying to decide how much the traffic will bear, and when do you price yourself out of the market."

Knowles had retired before the 1970s arrived, and the debates with the union centered around whether the annual wage increases should be 20 to 30 cents or 30 to 40 cents per hour. Or whether there should be two of them per year.

The Chambers Works was located in Salem County, and while this was a different Salem from the one in Massachusetts, which had a history of witch burning and other pious activities, the Salem in New Jersey also had a Puritan-type heritage. Most of the people who worked at the Chambers Works were honest, hard-working people with a solid respect for the Puritan ethic.

But not all of them respected the Puritan ethic. There are some crooks in every line of human endeavor, from archbishops and bartenders to xylophonists and zymologists, and some of them were at the Chambers Works.

One supervisor at the plant became famous for a scheme he cooked up which the Puritans would not have approved. He had a number of welders and mechanics reporting to him and he arranged to have these skilled craftsmen build a boat carrier for him using company materials and labor. He even paid them wage incentive for the time they spent on his pet project. It had wire wheels and a chassis long enough to carry a forty foot boat, and was a very handsome vehicle indeed—when he had it painted with Du Pont paint. He viewed it with great pride.

But when he attempted to haul it off the plant behind his automobile the guard on duty at the gate demanded that he show a pass signed by his superintendent giving him permission to remove one boat hauler. He had no such pass and so his pride and joy was confiscated on the spot. But this determined fellow was so attached to the carrier he had designed and constructed that he went to the plant manager and proposed that he be allowed to buy it. This permission was not granted and his handsome vehicle was dismantled by the same work force which had assembled it.

The supervisor was not fired because of this escapade, on the grounds that it had not succeeded, but he did lose his annual wage incentive bonus that year.

Another larcenous effort was directly concerned with dyes and it had a more unhappy ending for those involved.

The dye involved was Rhodamine B, one of the products that had helped give J. F. Darling and the basic colors area a reputation for being money-makers. Rhodamine B is a brilliant red, slightly phosphorescent dye with a bluish tint, which in those days had a variety of uses ranging from lipstick to high quality lithographic printing inks. Darling had installed facilities to make Rhodamine B and its cousin, Rhodamine 6GDN, in the Magenta Building after magenta itself had ceased to be profitable.

Du Pont, just before World War II, was the only manufacturer of Rhodamine B in the United States and a large part of the demand for this dye was supplied by imports from Germany. After Pearl Harbor the German source of supply was cut off and an acute shortage of the dye developed. The manufacture of Rhodamine B itself is not a complicated process but the basic intermediate used in the process, diethyl amino para cresol, requires special equipment to produce and neither Du Pont nor other domestic dye manufacturers could respond quickly to the shortage. So a black market demand for Rhodamine B quickly developed.

Du Pont rationed its shipments of Rhodamine B to established customers, in proportion to the amounts they had been buying before the shortage developed, and while this procedure left everyone somewhat unhappy there was no bitterness among the customers until a shipping clerk in the warehouse at Chambers Works decided to supply the black market demand in his own way.

He worked out an arrangement with a trucker who regularly hauled Chambers Works products to the New York area whereby they put an extra drum of Rhodamine B on the

truck, beyond what the shipping papers called for, and the
trucker delivered it to an ink maker who had no previous
record of purchases of this dye. The shipping clerk and the
trucker split the proceeds from this illegal transaction, and
all went well, they thought, for three or four months.

But several of Du Pont's established customers began
to complain that while they were unable to buy all the Rhodamine B they needed, a new competitor of theirs had no
supply problems and was taking lithographic ink business
from them. The New York sales office of Du Pont denied it
was selling to the newcomer but then one of the old customers took a Du Pont salesman to the newcomer's plant and
showed him two drums plainly marked "Du Pont Rhodamine
B." This led to an inventory audit of all Rhodamine B going
into and out of the warehouse at Chambers Works that disclosed a shortage of six drums worth about $10,000. Further
investigation came up with irrefutable evidence against the
shipping clerk who lost his job and went to jail for a short
term.

The boat carrier and Rhodamine B escapades, standing alone, would give a very misleading picture of the situation at Chambers Works. Of all the factors that may have
contributed to the eventual failure of the dye business, thiev-
ery probably was the most insignificant one of all. The account needs to be balanced by the story of Wilson Collins.

Wilson was a lanky middle-aged man with a long jaw
and the ambling walk of a farmer, which he had been, when
he came to work at the Chambers Works. He was a pillar of
the church in the small town where he lived, was highly regarded by his neighbors and was soon looked upon in the
same way by most of his associates at the plant.

The Chambers Works in those days had eight control
laboratories spread out over a thousand acres of land, and
these laboratories and related management offices had need
for frequent communication with each other. So an elaborate
mail system had been erected to meet that need. Twice each
day a special messenger carried letters, reports, analytical

results, and other materials to a total of about 25 locations.
Wilson was assigned to this messenger job and soon he was
doing it better than it had ever been done before. The mail
was always on time and it never went to the wrong location.

As already noted, Wilson's performance pleased most
of his associates. But not all of them. Wilson had some habits
that annoyed a few of the people he worked with.

He seldom wanted to stop by the "smoking corrals"
during the 15 minute rest periods alloted to all employees
twice a day, and when he did he made it known that he did
not want to hear any profanities or obscenities. This meant
he soon stopped visiting the smoking corrals entirely.

One day a superintendent of production was talking to
Wilson's supervisor when the lanky messenger walked briskly
by on one of his rounds. The superintendent had recently
heard some compliments about how well Wilson did his job
so he remarked to the supervisor that he was lucky to have
such a good man for the assignment.

"I don't know about that," the supervisor said. "He is a
damn nuisance in some ways. He lectures me every day about
smoking and tells me it is not only a dirty habit but is also
an unhealthy one. He is so pious he gets on the nerves of
some people and on top of that I think he is a hypocrite. He
tells everyone they should stop wasting time in the smoking
corrals and be sure to do eight hours' work for eight hours'
pay, but if you ever want to find him during a smoking period you can't. I suspect he goes somewhere and falls asleep,
and he sleeps longer than the others spend in the smoking
corral."

The superintendent challenged this estimate of Wilson
and said the supervisor was surely wrong about him sleeping
on the job.

"He moves too briskly when I see him and does his job
too well for that sort of thing," the superintendent said.

"I'll prove to you that he sneaks off and goes to sleep,"
the supervisor retorted. "Sometime next week I'll follow him
around and catch him red-handed."

So, the next week the supervisor did follow Wilson on his morning round of trips, and sure enough, when the smoking period arrived Wilson headed for a broom closet near the central cateteria, went inside and closed the door behind him. The supervisor waited for about ten minutes, to give Wilson time to go soundly asleep, then walked up to the closed door and suddenly pulled it open.

There stood Wilson leaning against a stack of brooms, with a single, dangling light bulb above him, holding an open Bible in his hands, and reading softly to himself.

"What did you do then?" the supervisor was asked.

"I shut that door as fast as I could and got the hell away from there," he replied.

Then the supervisor paused for a moment before adding, "And I believe that every other supervisor at Chambers Works would have done the same thing. That Book gave him perfect protection."

But no other book would have.

CRYSTAL VIOLET—
WINNER ALL
THE WAY

12

Crystal Violet probably has stained the hands of more people than any other dye in history, and also probably has been quietly cursed by more people than any other dye.

This is because it was the dye component in nearly all the "carbon paper" produced during the past seventy-five years, and millions of secretaries all over the world stained their fingertips, shirt fronts, and cuffs with this purple dye—until Xerox, IBM and others came along with duplicating systems which did not use crystal violet.

The first "carbon paper," as its name suggests, was made by mixing carbon black with waxes and then spreading a thin coat of this mixture on a sheet of paper. This carbon paper could then be used to make a "carbon copy" of a typewritten page. Or several copies could be made if several sheets of carbon paper were interleaved with plain paper and the typewriter keys were then struck with sufficient force. Carbon copies could also be made by hand using a sharp pencil or a stylus. These carbon copies were all black on white because black was the color of the carbon powder used in the wax.

Then along about the turn of the century someone conceived the idea of using finely divided crystal violet dye in place of the carbon black, and spreading a thin layer of this dye-wax mixture on a sheet to make a duplicating paper. This product might have been called "violet paper" or "purple paper," but the name of carbon paper had become so well established by then that the makers of the new product, and its users too, kept on calling the new duplicating paper by the old name of carbon paper.

The new carbon paper containing crystal violet had several advantages over the old product. It was easier to make three or four copies using the new carbon paper because the new product did not require as much pressure to make a legible copy and so the typewriter keys did not have to be struck so vigorously. Second, it was vastly easier to make thirty or forty copies because the crystal violet in each copy was soluble in alcohol (spirit) and so a clean sheet of paper could be moistened with alcohol and then pressed against a first copy thereby dissolving enough color to make a new legible copy. And the crystal violet was so strong tinctorially that the process could be repeated thirty or forty times before the dye on that first copy was exhausted. This process became known as "spirit duplication" and was very popular with teachers who wanted to pass out tests or other material to a class of thirty or forty. It still is widely used today in countries which are too poor to afford the relatively expensive duplicating machines put out by Xerox, IBM, Savin, and others.

The copies produced by crystal violet carbon paper using the spirit duplication process are, of course, violet in shade rather than black, but to some people, particularly those in tropical countries where violets and purples are common in nature, this vivid shade was more desirable than black. Others found the purple shade offensive but nearly everyone liked the convenience and low cost associated with the spirit duplication process for making multiple copies. However, not everyone liked the purple color that stained hands and clothing, so when Xerox came along most clerical workers welcomed it with great enthusiasm.

When the Du Pont Company started to manufacture crystal violet during the early 1920s this dye was already a very old product because the British and Germans had been making it for over fifty years. It was first used as a dye for wool and cotton but it failed in this application for several reasons. First, the rather garish purple color was too gaudy to suit many people, just as Perkin's mauve had been, but there were more important reasons. Crystal violet dyes fibers unevenly and it had miserable fastness to light and washing. After it failed as a dye for fabrics it was used in water and alcohol based soluble inks, but again poor light fastness was a problem. This problem was partly solved by reacting the soluble dye with phospho tungstic acid to make an insoluble pigment which was then ground with oils to make conventional oil based inks and paints. It was also used as a fungicide or bacteriocide and found other miscellaneous applications, but carbon paper and spirit duplication have consumed more crystal violet than all other uses combined.

Despite the half-century lead which the Germans and British had in the technology of crystal violet, during the period from 1920 to 1930 the Du Pont Company developed an improved grade of this old dye which performed so well in carbon paper and spirit duplication that it ran away from the field and became the world standard for this application. Furthermore, Du Pont's crystal violet maintained that position of leadership for fifty years—until 1980 when the company sold what remained of its dye business.

During this fifty year period crystal violet produced earnings in excess of twenty-five million dollars for Du Pont and always maintained a rate of return on investment well above the company average.

Accordingly, a case history study of crystal violet might be even more useful to students of business than an analysis of the deficiencies and omissions that eventually led to the death of Du Pont's entire dye business. One is a case history of success, the other a corresponding case history of failure.

The development that did more than any other one thing to push Du Pont's crystal violet to the top of the pyramid was a patent by James K. Reed claiming a new crystal structure for the dye. This new crystal structure was obtained by dissolving the dye in ethyl alcohol and then heating the mixture to evaporate off the alcohol. The inventor was the same man who was, at one time, J. F. Darling's chief assistant, and who later became general superintendent of all dye manufacture. He was also half of the famous Chambers Works team of humorous toastmasters—Reed and Fielding.

Reed and his associate in the sales division, Tom Martone, who did the testing and evaluation work, understood what Reed had done but many others, particularly the patent examiner, apparently did not. The examiner kept insisting that no invention was involved in the alcohol treatment since any impurities in the dye at the start were still present after the alcohol was evaporated. This statement was true, of course, but of no real significance. Reed had produced a new crystal type, not simply a purification, and his claim was eventually allowed. The resulting patent became the solid base upon which Du Pont built its crystal violet business. However, a patent lasts for only seventeen years and if Reed's invention had not been followed by a host of quality improvement and cost reduction programs, crystal violet almost certainly would have died before the whole Du Pont dye business did in 1980.

In fact, some of the improvements that kept crystal violet profitable for sixty years began before Reed's invention, and were a part of Du Pont's first efforts involving this dye.

While crystal violet is the simplest of all the triphenyl methane dyes it is nevertheless a complex organic chemical. And, as is usually the case with organic chemicals, there are several chemical paths that can be followed to arrive at the desired end product.

In the case of crystal violet there are at least half a dozen routes which can be followed in making it. The three most obvious to the chemist are: 1) the ketone process, 2) the hydrol process, and 3) the aldehyde process. Only the first two, the ketone and hydrol processes, were ever operated on a plant scale. Du Pont built plant facilities for both and operated both for over twenty-five years, before concluding that the ketone process gives better costs and better quality. The hydrol process survived as long as it did only because the dye produced this way did have some quality advantages in certain uses even though it was, on balance, inferior.

One major advantage of the ketone process lay in the fact that it permitted crystal violet to be manufactured with far less operating labor than the hydrol process required. In addition, it produced a dye that was inherently better suited to carbon paper and spirit duplication.

The labor savings in the ketone process resluted primarily from the fact that it permitted so many intermediate chemicals to be produced and used all in the same vessel without isolating these intermediates. The starting material, liquid dimethyl aniline, was pumped into a large reactor and then phosgene was added to produce dimethyl amino benzoyl chloride. This intermediate then reacted with excess dimethyl aniline to produce Michler's ketone, which gave the process its name. Still, without isolation, the Michler's ketone was reacted with another part of the excess dimethyl aniline to produce crystal violet itself. Then for the first time in this process a product was isolated—the desired dye. All this used about one-fifth as much labor as would have been required if all the intermediates had been isolated.

The subsequent filtering, washing, drying, alcohol treatment, grinding, and blending steps did require much labor, and these steps were the subjects of cost reduction studies that extended over a period of thirty years, ending in a process for which the last five stages were nearly as efficient as the first four already described. Continuous filtering devices and continuous drying equipment were critical parts of these labor-saving changes.

A measure of just how effective the labor-saving studies were is indicated by the fact that labor rates at the dye works increased, during the period from 1935 to 1975, by a factor of about twenty, while the labor costs required to make a hundred pounds of crystal violet increased by a factor of only two during that same period. This great reduction in operating labor costs also greatly reduced overhead costs, which were allocated in proportion to labor, and so overhead costs never did become, for crystal violet, the great burden that they were for nearly all other dyes.

Studies to reduce operating labor costs were only a small part of the sixty-year program of research and development designed to improve the crystal violet process. Quality improvement and quality control programs involved many more engineers and chemists than labor-saving studies did. Over the period from 1920 to 1980 nearly a hundred engineers and chemists were employed in these programs. Some of the people who contributed most were: Jim Reed, Edmund Humphrey, J. F. Darling, Harvey Stryker, E. S. Wierman, Richard Markham, Kenneth Whittle, and Donald Dietz.

Whittle, who directly supervised manufacture in the plant for over a quarter-century, made a study correlating chemical analyses with quality that greatly helped to define the composition of crystal violet that was best suited to carbon paper and spirit duplication.

The chemical structure usually written by chemists for crystal violet makes it look rather simple. It is not. More sophisticated formulae show that it is a salt of hydrochloric acid combined with a complex resonating ion consisting of three dimethyl amino phenyl groups attached to one central carbon atom, but even this is a great oversimplification.

For example, the crystal violet that Reed patented and caused to become the world standard for use in carbon paper always contained a small amount of zinc—from the step used to produce the Michler's ketone intermediate—and this zinc played a vital role in determining the quality of the final dye. Too much zinc caused the wax to mix poorly with the dye and too little zinc caused the later copies in spirit duplication to be weaker than was desired. Whittle studied this and similar problems for over twenty-five years and he came closer to being able to define the optimum exact chemical analysis than any other person did, but he never claimed to know the answer exactly. There were too many other factors that interacted with zinc content, such as the purity of the dimethyl aniline used at the start of the process, the reaction temperatures during the Michler's ketone and color formation steps—and dozens of other process variables. These many variables prevented him from ever being certain that he had the quality problem completely under control.

The business student studying this case history of an old product that remained profitable throughout the depression of the 1930s, the inflation of the 1970s, and all the intermediate stages between these two, is forced to conclude that continued research and development programs are as vital to an old product as they are to a new one. However, this conclusion does not provide a route to guaranteed success in the chemical business or perhaps any other.

Research programs can be mandated by management but success in the programs can not be mandated. Success comes only when the opportunities for it exist and even then only when the people involved are experienced and bright enough to recognize these opportunities and ingenious enough to put them in effect.

It must not be assumed from all this that the people working with crystal violet always knew what they were doing. For example, the patent examiner was not the only person who had trouble understanding just what Jim Reed accomplished by his alcohol treatment; someone in the dye hierarchy gave Reed's new product the official name of Du Pont Crystal Violet Extra Pure APN. Those last three letters in that name were taken from the phrase "Alcohol Purified New"!

13

JIM REED AND OTHER EXPLOSIONS

James K. Reed was born in 1893, and so was one year older than his partner in the famous toastmaster team of Reed and Fielding, that did so much to lighten and brighten retirement parties during the days of glory for dyes at the Chambers Works; but he appeared to be ten or fifteen years younger.

Reed's comparatively youthful appearance was due in part to Fielding's face which was as craggy as Mark Twain's, but was mostly due to the fact that Reed himself had a dapper youthful appearance throughout his career at the Chambers Works. His face was unlined, his hair was still all there, he maintained a well-trimmed small mustache, and his eyes sparkled. Jay Pratt said he had "a dancing little devil in each eye!"

Because he served as general superintendent of manufacture for all dyes and intermediate chemicals Reed was well known all over the Chambers Works but he was even better known for his explosions. He would explode with laughter at the punch line of a funny story, whether he was listening to it or telling it, and he would explode with anger when someone said or did something which he thought was stupid beyond the call of duty.

Consequently, people went out of their way to tell him

Jim Reed was general superintendent of manufacture for dyes and their intermediates when the business was a very healthy one. He is shown here holding the binoculars just handed to him by his chief assistant, J. C. Kinahan, on the occasion of a testimonial dinner for Reed on the 35th anniversary of his joining the Du Pont Company.

jokes, and they tried to get out of the way when he became angry.

The engineering division at the Chambers Works produced more than its fair share of stupidities, in Reed's opinion, so nearly all of the maintenance engineers tried to steer clear of him when something went wrong with a new installation, or repairs fell behind schedule. An exception to this rule was Lou Marcotte, the chief engineer, who was an expert at defusing explosive situations involving Reed and the engineers, a number of whom thought Reed was a wild man.

"Hell," Marcotte said, "Jimmy is a reasonable man. He wants to get the work done right and he gets hot in a hurry if it isn't done that way, but if you give him a few seconds to blow off steam, or you duck behind the desk when he can't get the relief valve open fast enough, everything will be back to normal in a minute or two, and then there isn't a more sensible man in the plant."

Reed's explosions occurred at all levels in the organization but he practically never abused those far down the line, and his most violent explosions were provoked by contacts with those above him. Asked one day why he behaved this way, Reed grinned and said: "I can't expect too much from a second-class operator or a junior supervisor, but a man in high position should know better. There is no excuse for a sales manager or a production manager being as stupid as some of them are."

Reed and Dr. E. C. Humphrey, who always outranked him by a level or two, were friends for many years and Reed certainly did not think Humphrey was stupid, but all that did not prevent an explosion in Humphrey's Wilmington office one day. These two experts on dyes were talking along pleasantly enough when the subject of sales complaints about dye quality came up and Humphrey apparently forgot he was talking to the man who had invented the most successful dye Du Pont ever manufactured, Crystal Violet Extra Pure APN.

"Jim," Humphrey said, "we are having all these complaints about APN simply because we have neglected research on crystal violet for many years now."

Reed leaped to his feet.

"Doc," he said, "that is a lot of damn nonsense and you know it, and I'm not going to sit here and listen to it."

And with that he picked up his briefcase and headed for the door. Whereupon, Humphrey rose also and said in a pleading tone: "Wait a minute, Jim. We have been friends too long for you to rush away mad like this."

Reed was only partly placated.

"I know we have been friends for thirty years," he said, "but that doesn't mean I have to sit here and listen to a lot of damn foolishness all day long."

This remark released the steam which had heated him up and then he grinned and said: "All right. I'll come back, but I'm going to leave my briefcase here by the door so I can get away in a hurry if I have to."

But the storm was over and the two old experts on triphenyl methane dyes settled back in their chairs and began to talk about the old days when crystal violet was struggling to establish itself in the world markets for carbon paper.

"The quality in those days was not half as good as it is now," Reed said, "but we had a lot fewer complaints from the sales division."

"That's right, Jim," Humphrey said. "I'm going to tell Charlie Schaumann the sales division should do more selling and less bellyaching."

By this time Reed had recovered completely. "Good Lord, Doc," he said. "That is the first time I ever heard you side with the plant in an argument with the sales division about quality."

Reed's explosions were not all verbal. Despite the incredible amount of attention which he and members of his supervisory force devoted to matters of safety, some physical explosions did occur in his manufacturing areas. Some oc-

Jim Reed and Ed Fielding were toastmasters at many testimonial dinners for Chambers Works people. When a dinner was held for Reed himself he joined in the fun and happily wore a top hat after a mock convention nominated him for president. The garbled state names shown on the placards represent areas of the plant under his management. "Azorina," for example, represented the Azo colors area which produced more pounds of dyes than any other area.

curred because of human errors, but others resulted from hazards that were so subtle even the most attentive and well trained chemists could not anticipate them.

The explosion in the para nitro benzoyl chloride (PNB chloride) distillation vessel was an example of the subtle hazards that lurked in many places on a plant where over a thousand complex organic chemicals were manufactured. PNB chloride had been distilled safely for over ten years when it blew up one night, sending the lid of the still up through the roof of the crystal violet building and driving the body of this 1500 gallon vessel into the concrete of the floor below where it had been installed.

Fortunately, no one was injured, chiefly because the operator in charge of the vessel had heard a rumbling in the receiver of the still and had fled the building, taking the operator on the floor below along with him. The big blow came a minute or so later.

In the investigation which followed someone suggested that the operator might have prevented the explosion if he had investigated the ominous noise he had heard, and so he should be officially reprimanded.

Reed interrupted instantly and his eyes were flashing when he said: "Reprimand hell! He should be commended. I want a note of official commendation put in his personnel file saying he did just what he should have done. And I want special mention made of the fact that he took the operator on the floor below along with him when he went. We can replace a busted kettle but not an operator."

At first no explanation as to why the kettle had blown up was possible. The log sheets showed that the operator had loaded the right materials into it and the temperature chart showed it had been heated up according to standard procedures. After about ten days of investigation, it turned out that the explosion had occurred because the PNB acid used as the starting material for PNB chloride had contained about 10% of ONB acid as an impurity. These two materials, PNB acid and ONB acid, look alike and so do the PNB chloride and ONB chloride made from them. But the PNB chloride can be distilled safely while the ONB chloride decomposes violently when it is heated up. Unfortunately, this information had not been recorded anywhere in the literature of chemistry up to that time.

Reed attended the final review on the explosion and commended the chemist who had made the discovery about the explosive nature of ONB chloride, but he did it in his own fashion.

"It is about time you did something to earn your salary," he said. "Up to now you have been the highest paid man at the Chambers Works, when consideration is given to what you do for what you get paid."

The devils in Reed's eyes were dancing merrily when he delivered this left-handed compliment, and no one there misunderstood him. So no one was surprised when he promoted the chemist a few weeks later.

Reed said frequently that he was always pleased when investigation showed that some mishap was caused by ignorance and not stupidity. "We have more than enough ignorance in the chemical industry," he said, "but ignorance can be cured by research while stupidity stays with a man as long as he lives."

Another explosion in one of Reed's areas did involve a human error. This explosion was vastly greater than the one in the PNB chloride vessel. It occurred when an operator mistakenly loaded a drum of dinitro phenol into a vessel and heated it up instead of using beta naphthol as the instructions called for.

The resulting explosion blew off one corner of the manufacturing building and pieces of flying steel penetrated other buildings and started fires there. One piece of steel punctured a tank car of naphthalene standing nearby and set fire to the contents of the car. This fire led to other fires and before fire chief Royden Sparks got them all under control the damage amounted to about a million and a half dollars.

The burning naphthalene caused a plume of fire and smoke several hundred feet high which attracted attention in Wilmington and Philadelphia. So the newspapers in these two cities dispatched reporters to the Chambers Works to find out what the trouble was, but by the time they arrived the fires were under control and they could not see much. So the reporters wanted to come inside the gates to inspect the damage up close.

Both Reed and Frank Knowles, the plant manager,

were adamant in refusing to permit the reporters inside the gates of the plant.

"We have enough trouble," Reed said, "without having a flock of reporters who don't know benzene from sulfuric acid under foot. They would probably kill themselves and if they didn't do that they might kill us."

The reporters were persistent but finally gave up and sent word they would settle for an estimate of the dollar value of the damage done. No one had made any real estimate of the damage at that point but it must have been as obvious to Reed as it was to others on the scene that the cost of repairs would be somewhere around a million dollars, possibly two million dollars.

Reed had slept very little the previous night and had been in the plant since about 3:00 a.m. It was then close to noon and his face had an uncharacteristic look of weariness, but when he began to think about what estimate of damages he should give the reporters a trace of the twinkle, which usually lurked in his eyes suddenly reappeared.

"Tell them," he said, "the damage may run as high as ten thousand dollars."

SAM BAKER

14

reat God in the morning, Sam," the Senator said, "I almost went home to Oklahoma. They told me a general manager from Du Pont was coming to see me and I couldn't have cared less. Why didn't they say the brightest guy in the whole company, and the second best cribbage player in the world was coming to see me?"

This was the way U. S. Senator Robert Kerr, the Oklahoma oil man and multi-millionaire, greeted Sam Baker when Baker headed a group that was doing some lobbying on tariffs for the Synthetic Organic Chemical Manufacturers Association (SOCMA), a few years after Baker succeeded Jack Daley as general manager of the organic chemicals department.

It was during the Daley and Baker reigns that dyes achieved their most extended period of high profitability, and the exceptional executive ability of these two men was a strong factor in this period of success for dyes. Their styles were different but both were shrewd managers and both had an amazing ability to sweep aside unessential details to get to the heart of a problem. Baker, in particular, seemed to react instinctively but as he himself said on many occasions sound instincts are just an indication of sound basic intelligence.

It should be noted that not everyone in the Du Pont

Samuel Garland Baker was general manager of the organic chemicals department when dyes had some of their very best years. (Photography by Willard Stewart.)

Company agreed with Senator Kerr's evaluation of Sam Baker. Even Baker himself took exception to part of it.

"What does that damn Kerr mean by calling me the second best cribbage player in the world?," he said later to one of his associates in the lobbying group. "He knows perfectly well that I'm the best cribbage player in the world. He likes to think he is, but I beat him six or seven times out of every ten times I play him. I'm not even sure he is the second best."

All this was typical of the kind of bantering which Baker loved to engage in with oil company customers back in the days when his new department was consistently first or second in earnings—plus rate of return on investment in the Du Pont Company. He was a natural salesman who instructed everyone to call him Sam and he got along superbly with all customers but particularly well with millionaire customers such as Senator Kerr, of the Kerr-McGee Oil Company, which bought more tetra ethyl lead (TEL) from Du Pont than from the other two competitors combined.

"Too many people in Du Pont," Sam said, "fail to understand how difficult selling is and how important it is. But it does no good to develop new products or to manufacture them if they don't get sold. Customers tend to buy from people they like, and they like people who appear to be enjoying themselves."

Using this definition of a good salesman, it was clear that Sam himself was a magnificent one. He liked nearly everyone he met and he enjoyed himself with all classes of people from shoeshine boys to U.S. senators—but millionaire oil men were his favorites. Consequently, he spent a little more time with customers of the TEL division than he did with those of dyes and "Freon" refrigerants. This was partly because he liked the oil men so much, and partly because his instincts told him he could increase departmental earnings more that way.

Sam never ignored the research and manufacturing divisions in his new department, but he quickly sensed that these groups were well established in a routine which did not require much of his attention.

He made a quick survey of the manufacturing processes at Chambers Works and announced that he had learned all he needed to know about TEL and "Freon" in one day inspection trips devoted to each. Dyes were another matter.

"I want to spend a day a week for the next two months," he told the assistant manager at Chambers Works, "going through the dyes and intermediates areas so I can get a feeling for what you are doing and why you are doing it the way you do. Daley told me that you people over here were always throwing six-sided benzene rings at him and all it did was confuse him. It won't bother me because I have no intention of learning the chemical formulas for all your dyes, but I do want to learn why you make every lot different from the previous one."

He paused at this point and grinned. "At least that is what the people in sales tell me you do."

When Sam embarked on his program of learning how dyes were made he took the assistant manager of the plant with him on all his visits, and explained this action in typical Baker fashion.

"I want somebody along," he said, "who can introduce me and answer some questions, but I don't want to take Frank Knowles because he has important work to do. So you can fill in for him. He tells me you don't do much anyway."

He knew that this request to have the assistant manager accompany him was a flattering one and he also knew that it would flatter the supervisors, foremen, and operators when he insisted on meeting them in each building he visited. Also, the total attention that he gave to every man he talked with was flattering to men who seldom met anyone higher in the organization than the area superintendent. When he asked a question it was never a perfunctory one. He wanted to know the answer and he listened to it with total attention. He was particularly interested in "know how" details which were not spelled out in written procedures which the operators followed.

When he was told that the process for making ethyl ketone involved a "graining" technique that only one operator in the plant could carry out successfully, he immediately wanted to meet that operator, Dominic Damato.

"Dominic," he said, "I'm told you are the only man in the Chambers Works who can grain ethyl ketone and that other people can watch you do it and they still can't figure out how you do it. Show me what you do."

"There ain't much to it, Mr. Baker," Dominic started out.

"Call me Sam," was the instant reply. He then watched with intense attention while Dominic proceeded to cool down a slurry of water and molten ethyl ketone. At the proper moment Dominic shut off the agitation, cooled it some more, started agitation again briefly, and finally looked at Sam with a triumphant smile when the liquid mass suddenly formed tiny grains of solid ethyl ketone.

"Why did you decide just when you did to stop the agitation and when to start it again, Dominic?" Sam asked.

"When it looks just right I stop it, and when it looks just right again I start agitation again," Dominic replied.

Sam grinned. "I see," he said. "What happens when someone else tries to do it?"

"It usually comes down in big balls or one big chunk," Dominic said, "and then it is a tough job to wash the impurities out of it on the nutsch."

After eight sessions of inspection in the dye areas Sam announced that he knew as much as he needed to know about how dyes were made.

"I won't live long enough to learn all the details about dye manufacture," he told his escort, "so I'll leave all that to you people who have grown up in the business. But I do have a feeling now for how complicated the manufacture of dyes is. I know that much of it has never been written down and probably can't be because people like Dominic Damato can't tell you exactly what they do and why they do it. It is just a feel, a sort of instinct coupled with experience. I came over here to learn enough about what you do so that I will be able to recognize baloney when someone tries to feed it to me. Now I think I can—most of the time anyway."

Samuel Garland Baker was a man with a great many interests, many related to business and many others entirely separated from it, but he pursued all of them with an enthusiasm which was amazing. His enthusiasms included, among many others, reading, hunting, and the United States Naval Academy.

Sam hunted birds—mostly ducks, geese, partridge and rail birds—all over the world but mostly up and down the Atlantic Coast. One of his favorite foreign countries was Spain where he went to shoot partridge. After one of his expeditions to Spain he returned with four dozen red-legged partridge and held a dinner at the Wilmington Club for high ranking members of the research, manufacturing, and sales divisions of his department. In addition to partridge, the dinner featured German white wine from the Mosel River. Mosel wine was another of his enthusiasms and he never drank anything else when it was available. In fact, during his association with dyes Sam never drank any hard liquors. When "good white wine," meaning Mosel wine, was not available he drank only beer.

During the partridge dinner at the Wilmington Club several of his guests congratulated Sam on the excellence of the food and wine.

"Of course, it is the best," he replied, "because the best is scarcely good enough for us."

To make sure he would not run out of Mosel wine Sam frequently imported large quantities of it. On one occasion a big shipment arrived at his house when only his daughter, Janet, was at home. Sam's next door neighbor, Monty Smith, saw Janet directing the truckers where to store the large number of cardboard boxes and asked her what it was.

"It's Daddy's wine," Janet replied.

Sam Baker loved to go hunting. Here he is shown ready to shoot quail. When the food and wine were at their best he reminded his guests that "The best is scarcely good enough for us."

"Good Lord," Monty said, "how much did he order?"

"I didn't count it," Janet replied, "but I signed a receipt for fifty-four cases. Daddy gets thirsty a lot."

However, Sam did not drink all the wine he imported. He gave away a lot of it to friends and customers of Du Pont, such as oil company presidents and vice-presidents who went with him on gunning trips.

Reading was one of Sam's enthusiasms which surprised many people who thought he was too busy hunting, playing cribbage and gin rummy, and going to athletic contests to have time for anything else. Nevertheless, he did find time for reading and he read so rapidly that he would consume a three hundred page book in a single night. He once read an account of John Brown's raid at Harper's Ferry and reported that "I finished it in about two hours and was panting with excitement for the last half hour. The author knew how to write."

Sam was fascinated by T. H. White's *The Once and Future King*. When Lerner and Loewe wrote the musical comedy, *Camelot,* based upon it he went to see the show twice within a single month. The first time he went with his wife, Frances, and the second time he took a bus load of high ranking managers and their wives, from the organic chemicals department. His wife objected mildly to going to see *Camelot* twice in the same month but she had learned long ago that the tide of Sam's enthusiasm was hard to swim against. Later she said she enjoyed the show more the second time, particularly the dinner at Sardi's Restaurant.

Sam's favorite author of all was Shakespeare and he said he enjoyed reading the plays more than seeing them on the stage. "Actors often get in the way of what Shakespeare had to say," was the way he explained his preference for the written word.

Throughout his time in the organic chemicals department Sam kept himself available to the three sales divisions on an almost equal time basis, with TEL slightly preferred. He gave manufacturing and research much less time.

"I know that research and manufacturing are important," he said, "and they will roll along pretty well anyway but when sales stop everything stops."

While Sam tried to treat the three sales division about equally, TEL usually came first, dyes second, and "Freon" third. TEL came first not because the product line was interesting but because it could produce more money and the customers were mostly millionaires whom he liked. Dyes came second because the colorful product line fascinated him and there were a few millionaires among the customers. "Freon" came third because the product line was as colorless as TEL and the millionaire customers were very rare.

However, Sam was delighted when "Freon" aerosol sales came up with a slogan which read: "The Spray is the Thing." When he first heard it his eyes sparkled and he said: "Great. The play's the thing wherein I'll catch the conscience of the king."

Then he added: "Tell your advertising people I like it when they use Shakespeare to help us sell. He is a better writer than any at B.B.D. & O. and we don't have to pay him any royalties because he has been in the public domain for a century or two."

There were three directors of sales for dyes during Sam's time in the organic chemicals department and of the three Bill Bours was clearly his favorite. The two of them carried on the kind of bantering which appealed to Sam, with Bours calling him "our almost peerless leader." Sam retaliated by insulting Bill's undergraduate school, Princeton, up to the limits of good taste or perhaps even beyond those limits. Sam did not resent the term "our almost peerless leader" if the tone was correct, and Bours was careful to keep it that way.

D. C. (Boony) Newman, who preceded Bill Bours as sales director for dyes, was the man who started a promotional scheme which made Du Pont somewhat famous—or infamous—during the 1950s and early 1960s.

This promotional scheme involved colored shirts, one shade for each day in the week. Newman insisted that his entire sales force wear these colored shirts at all times earlier than 6:00 p.m., and Sam enthusiastically supported him in this effort to regiment the sales force. White shirts were then the standard for business executives, but Newman enforced his program with a combination of good-humored persuasion and veiled threats so that soon all the aspiring young executives in the department were wearing colored shirts. For the most part other departments did not follow Newman's lead but the idea nevertheless got around that Du Pont required its executives to wear colored shirts. Even the *Wall Street Journal* took note of this belief.

One day at an executive committee lunch Sam was seated at the same table with Crawford Greenewalt who asked Sam about the colored shirt promotion.

"Sam," he said, "do you really think that our pushing colored shirts does much to promote the use of dyes?"

"I doubt it very much," Sam replied. "But this was Boony Newman's idea and he is enthusiastic about it. I like enthusiasm in a sales division so I help him with it whenever I can. I don't think it does any harm."

Sam paid serious attention to all sales complaints about quality and usually sided with the sales people when they complained that poor quality was costing them business. But he was aware of the fact that sales people tend to complain about quality whenever they lose business and practically never attribute the loss to poor performance in selling.

During one period the sales division lodged a long series of complaints about the quality of crystal violet and Sam finally called a group of manufacturing managers to discuss the situation.

"We have the best crystal violet in the world," they told him. "If we didn't we would not have 60% of the world's business even though most of our competitors sell at lower prices."

Sam was amazed at this claim and promptly called Gordon Markle of the sales division in to discuss it.

"The manufacturing people tell me," he said to Markle, "that we have 60% of all the business and charge a premium price, but I gather from the reports of your sales offices that we have an inferior product. Is that the way you understand it too?"

Markle blinked and said, "We don't claim it is inferior. We say it is inconsistent and sometimes inferior."

Sam grinned: "Well," he said, "it must not be inferior most of the time unless we have the best damn sales force in the world. Tell your boys they should do more selling and less complaining."

The meeting ended with Sam and all those present in a high good humor, but for one reason or another the number of complaints about crystal violet suddenly became greatly reduced.

Sam was a member of the Class of 1923 at the Naval Academy and withdrew in his last year there, partly under pressure and partly because of his own convictions concerning a squabble about the hazing of plebes, but he never lost his enthusiasm for and loyalty to the Navy. He frequently organized trips to Annapolis to see Navy play football and lacrosse and when the Academy built a new football stadium there after World War II he donated enough money to construct Gate 23 and install the seats in section 23 of the new stadium. After that all his parties were required to enter the stadium through Gate 23 regardless of where their seats were located.

When Sam retired from Du Pont in 1963 all three divisions of the organic chemicals department had finished several years of great prosperity and Sam told his successor, Bill Kay, that "there is no place for this department to go except down."

It was one of the few times that he predicted incorrectly because the organic chemicals department, and dyes in particular, had several excellent years under Kay. However, as time went by Sam's prediction began to come true and dyes slid sharply under Kay's successor, Carl Oldach. The good years became scarce, particularly for dyes, and they were even scarcer under Oldach's successor, Roy Schuyler.

And by the time Bob Blair was put in charge of dyes even a good month was a rarity.

Sam did not live to see the death of the dye business and he never criticized his successors during the declining years of the 1970s, but often insisted that inflation had made it difficult to manage any business—dyes in particular because Chambers Works had the highest wage rates in the Du Pont Company.

His concern about inflation had been one of long standing and he complained about it even during the early 1960s when it amounted to only two or three percent per year. He instructed the purchasing agents assigned to his department to exert every pressure possible to keep down prices for the things they bought. He once urged the research division to study the manufacture of ethylene dibromide, which was purchased outside, in an effort to bluff the supplier into thinking that Du Pont would soon manufacture its own requirements. And he was delighted when the bluff worked. However, he had a different point of view concerning sales prices for dyes, TEL, and "Freon" and urged the sales directors to test the market constantly to see if higher prices could be obtained.

When Sam was reminded that he had a split personality when it came to prices he grinned and said: "I always see both sides of every question but that doesn't mean I have to be impartial on all matters."

Tariffs were another matter on which Sam saw both sides of the question before coming down squarely on one side. He was one of the most vigorous and articulate presidents which SOCMA ever had when it came to supporting high tariffs to protect the dye business. One of his speeches on the subject caused a chemist in Jackson Laboratory to write him a letter saying that tariff protection was not needed by Du Pont's dye business which should rely upon the scientists in Jackson Laboratory to keep dyes sufficiently ahead of all foreign competition. He added that free trade was good for everyone.

Sam snorted when he read the letter and every time he discussed it with the research and manufacturing managers in Wilmington.

"I know," he said, "that free trade is a good thing in general, but the dye business could never have survived against German competition during the 1920s without tariff protection. Even today, after Du Pont has thirty years of experience and know how it would be pushed right against the wall without protection because the Germans have eighty years of experience. We have the same kind of chemists the German have—some bright and some stupid. I suspect this guy is one of our stupid ones. He doesn't seem to understand that his own salary would be half what it is today and wages at the Chambers Works would be a third what they are, if there were any jobs at all, without tariff protection.

"I know free trade is good for everyone and I'm all for it, but free trade means more than just tariffs. I suppose I should tell this poor sap about import licenses, quotas, and government subsidies to foreign competitors or maybe I should just fire him. But I don't think I'll do either one. Life is too short and I have to do some goose hunting."

Although Sam's batting average was an amazingly high one he did not succeed in everything he tried. One of his failures came in his extended battle against inflation and involved Wilbur the shoeshine boy who really was a middle-aged black man named Wilbert Adams. Everyone called him Wilbur and Wilbur went along with that name with amused good humor. Perhaps like all good businessmen he felt compelled to cater to the whims of his customers wherever this was possible.

Wilbur was a friend of Henry B. du Pont and through Henry he had obtained the shoeshine franchise for the Du Pont and Nemours buildings. That is to say, he was the only man permitted to take his shoebox into the offices of all the executives and shine their shoes on the spot.

For many years Wilbur had charged twenty-five cents for a shoe shine and it was a good price when he first started his business. But as the years went by, even the moderate inflation of the 1950s and early 1960s eroded its value so in 1962 Wilbur decided to raise his price to thirty cents.

Shortly thereafter Wilbur came into Sam's office without knocking, as was his custom, and found Sam conducting a meeting with some manufacturing managers on the subject of TEL manufacture. Both sales and production of TEL were proceeding well at the time and Sam was in fine good humor, partly for that reason and partly because his secretary had just come in to remind him that he was scheduled to have lunch with his daughter, Mary Bacon, and to give Mary a birthday present for his granddaughter, Betsy Bacon.

"Come in, Wilbur," Sam said, "and go right to work. After you finish my shoes I think there is a dollar's worth of business available with the others here."

So Wilbur spread his pad on the floor and started to work on Sam's shoes, but when he had nearly finished the first shoe he paused, looked up, and said: "Mr. Baker, everything has been going up in price lately and I ain't had a raise in ten years so I have decided to raise my price for a shoe shine to thirty cents."

"Stop right there, Wilbur," Sam said with vigor. "This business of inflation has got to be stopped at every point and I'm not going to pay thirty cents for a shoe shine."

So Wilbur did stop in obvious dismay.

"But, Mr. Baker," he said. "I have already told a lot of my customers that the new price is thirty cents and they have all accepted it."

"I can't help that," Sam replied. "You can charge them whatever you like but I'm not going to pay more than a quarter."

Wilbur's look of dismay increased and he was obviously shaken. Finally he said: "Mr. Baker, I can't have two prices in the same building."

When Wilbur finished this clear statement of the Robinson-Patman law Sam broke into a wide smile.

"I guess you are right about that," he said, "but I still

can't pay thirty cents for a shoe shine so I'll tell you what I will do. I'll bet you ten dollars, even money, that the Phillies win the pennant this year, but you will have to shine my shoes for a quarter the rest of the year."

The Phillies were then in last place and had not finished in the first division for five years, all of which both Sam and Wilbur knew. Wilbur also knew a good thing when he saw it so he promptly accepted the bet and just as promptly proceeded to shine Sam's other shoe. Wilbur won the bet, of course, and the next year Sam paid thirty cents just like all Wilbur's other customers.

Some years later, when inflation had increased from the two or three percent of that time up to double digit figures one of the men present that day recalled Sam's attempt to curb inflation in the shoe shine business.

"It all goes to show," he said, "that no one has been able to control inflation. Not even the great Sam Baker."

A RARE BIRD

15

Before I introduce him to you I would like to tell you that the President of the Du Pont Company and I have an agreement. I don't write any books and he doesn't shoot any birds. This is partly because he is a rare bird himself."

This was the way Sam Baker introduced Crawford H. Greenewalt to a group of important customers in the du Barry Room of the Hotel du Pont one day during the period when both dyes, and the whole Du Pont Company were riding high. And if the picture then in vogue of a corporation executive was nearly correct, Baker was certainly right in calling Greenewalt a rare bird.

For half a century or so the general public, particularly in literate and academic circles, had been harboring the belief that corporation executives were one dimensional fellows interested in nothing except making money and they never read anything except balance sheets and perhaps the *Wall Street Journal.* They were thought to be shrewd enough but were also assumed to be almost illiterate. If one of them released a piece of writing under his signature it was generally believed that someone in the public relations department had written it for him. H. L. Mencken stated the general public's idea of businessmen when he said: "It is, after all, a sound instinct which puts business below the professions, and burdens the businessman with a social inferiority that he can never quite shake off, even in America. . . . He is the only man above the hangman and scavenger who is forever apologizing for his occupation."

Greenewalt, at the time Sam Baker introduced him to the group of customers, had been splashing paint all over this picture of the businessman for many years. He had shown clearly that he was a many-sided man with an astonishing array of interests beyond the balance sheet even though he must have given a lot of attention to Du Pont's balance sheet because it was then a thing of beauty and a joy to the stockholders.

Greenewalt was a scientist who was at ease with plutonium plants, benzene rings, the copper phthalocyanine blues and greens, the crystallinity of stretched nylon, and the nature of the colors which give the hummingbird its brilliant hues. But the arts and literature also interested him intensely and he not only read books, he wrote them too.

One of his books, *The Uncommon Man,* had become a best seller and its graceful language must have caused readers to believe that if some public relations man had written it then Du Pont had a truly uncommon man in that department.

Another book, *Hummingbirds,* was the artistic and scientific hit of the decade and its publication caused nearly everyone to give up the notion that the public relations department was doing Greenewalt's writing. In the introduction to this book he rolled out phrases such as "gape not deeply cleft," and dozens of others with a fine Shakespearean swing which could have stretched most public relations men past their breaking point. And when he went on to explain the physics of interference colors it must have been plain to all that the public relations department was not present even as a distant echo.

Then when *Bird Song* was published it was so loaded with the physics of sound and the physiology of bird larynxes that book reviewers all over the country threw up their hands in surrender and left this book to the scientists. However,

Ensifera Ensifera. This rare bird, which lives high in the mountains of Ecuador, was photographed and described by Crawford Greenewalt in his book on hummingbirds.

Crawford H. Greenewalt was president of the Du Pont Company when dyes and the whole Company were highly profitable. He had a hand in the change which moved Jack Daley from the pigments to the organic chemicals department when both departments were making "Monastral" colors. (Photograph courtesy of the Public Affairs Department, E. I. du Pont de Nemours & Company.)

before the surrender one reviewer, who had also read *Hummingbirds,* did say much the same thing that Sam Baker said. He declared that Greenewalt himself was as rare a bird as the swordbilled hummingbird, *Ensifera,* which Greenewalt had photographed high in the mountains of Ecuador. The beak of the *Ensifera* is longer than the rest of its body.

While the dye business had its most extended period of high profitability under Baker as general manager and Greenewalt as President neither one of these men got involved in the details of dye manufacture. Baker declared, "I will not live long enough to learn all the tricks of the dye business so I won't try." In addition he was deeply involved in tetra ethyl lead sales and to a lesser extent with "Freon" so he did not really have too much time for dyes. Greenewalt was even more busy with such things as the General Motors divestiture, the ICI suit, the expansion of nylon, and a few thousand other items, but he and Baker shared at least a few points in common when it came to management philosophy.

Baker came into an Orchem staff meeting one day and announced to the group that "Yesterday I heard the most encouraging thing I have heard in over thirty years with Du Pont."

He went on to say that he had eaten lunch with Greenewalt and some security analysts the day before and one of the analysts had asked if Du Pont used psychological testing to determine which of its executives was ready for advancement. Greenewalt had said "no," and added that numbers simply were not useful in such decisions.

"Well, then," the man asked, "how do you decide who should advance when an opening occurs?"

"Some way, somehow," Greenewalt replied, "outstanding ability becomes evident. I can't tell you any more about it than that."

Baker then told his staff group that all such decisions must be made by intuition which he said "is just another name for the combination of high basic intelligence and past experiences which are too vague and apparently not related to the problem to be defined in any precise way. Nearly all major decisions have to be based on intuition and every decision to start a new business is an intuitive one. There are no trend lines for a new business and even in an old business if the trend lines point to something which doesn't make sense a good businessman has to let his intuition override the trend lines."

Greenewalt visited the Chambers Works very infrequently so he never had much direct contact with people running the dye business in the plant, but he did have an important influence on the kind and amount of research done on dyes. He was a strong believer in the necessity for research and when the government caused Du Pont and ICI to discontinue their reciprocal research effort he said the decision might force the organic chemicals department to double its research on dyes. Greenewalt also sat in on reviews of segments of the dye business from time to time when they were presented to the Executive Committee of the Board of Directors.

One of these reviews involved the "Monastral" blues and greens and Baker gave the small group scheduled to make the presentation some advice before the review began.

"If the Committee members ask a question," he said, "answer it if you have the facts, but if you don't know, say so. There are two or three members of the Committee who think they know more about 'Monastral' colors than I do and they probably are right but they still don't know much. However, Greenewalt will be there and he can smell bull from as far away as any man I ever met. And he listens. If you make some idiotic prediction he will hear what you say and next year he will probably ask you about it."

This ability to listen to what was being said around him was a characteristic which Greenewalt carried into other areas of interest outside business. Because of the speeches he made and because of his books and other publications Greenewalt received a great many awards and honors from academic institutions. These honors included a score or so of honorary degrees and enough medals to make him look like General MacArthur on parade day, if he had worn them all at one time.

On one occasion when he went to receive a medal, a lady poet was also present to receive an honorary degree. When the college dean read the citation justifying her degree he called proper attention to the poet's skill with words, but added that she was also skilled in the kitchen and had once won first prize in a national contest for soup recipes. This bit of information brought a short laugh from the audience but probably was dismissed from memory rather promptly by most people who heard it. Greenewalt, however, went home and wrote the poet asking for a copy of her prize winning recipe. She sent it, and he said it made a pretty good soup.

In the days when he was the chief executive officer of Du Pont Greenewalt was asked to make a lot of speeches and they all had the cadence and balanced flow of words which characterized his books and even his table conversation. Nevertheless, some members of the press persisted in the belief that someone else must be writing his speeches even after the book reviewers and college presidents had long ago concluded that he did indeed write his own stuff.

One night after he addressed an assemblage of engineers in Philadelphia a man who identified himself as being from the *Evening Bulletin,* which nearly everyone in Philadelphia read in those days, put the question to him directly:

"Mr. Greenewalt," he said, "do you write your own speeches?"

"Mr. Altman," Greenewalt replied, "I am forced to confess that I do."

A rare bird.

THE ANATOMY
OF A FAILURE

16

The Du Pont Company's dye business lost money during the first ten years of its existence, from 1917 to 1927, and again during its last ten years, from 1970 to 1980.

However, during the intervening period of about forty years it made money and the total profits exceeded the total loses by over fifty million dollars. Just exactly what the accumulated profits were is hard to say because the dye business balance sheet was combined with a series of related products such as intermediates, textile finishing agents, rubber chemicals, and surfactants that varied from year to year.

Also, there came out of Jackson Laboratory, which started as a dye research center, a series of highly profitable products that included tetra ethyl lead, "Freon" products, "Teflon," neoprene, and other smaller products, which, in all, have produced earnings in excess of a billion dollars, with the total still growing each year. In addition, less direct branches of the organic chemicals industry, which for Du Pont got started in Jackson Laboratory, led to even more important product lines such as nylon, "Dacron," "Orlon," "Mylar," "Cronar," and other less well known but profitable items in the field of polymers.

In view of all this it might be argued that the Du Pont dye business, which died in 1980, was not a failure at all but a fantastic success story.

There is a certain amount of persuasiveness to this claim but not enough to make it really valid. It does not explain away the fact that the dye business eventually died at Du Pont but continued at other companies. The world is still buying as much dye materials as it ever did, perhaps even more. There was a competitive failure that was not the sort of thing that occurred when the buggy whip and leather harness business died. Du Pont's decision to sell the dye business and leave the field was not a philosophical one; it was a classic dollars and cents decision. Du Pont ceased to be able to manufacture and sell dyes at a profit, so competition took the business away, bit by bit at first, and finally in great gulps by purchase of large segments of the remaining dye business.

So, in at least a narrow sense, the dye business was eventually a failure, and the question to be answered is: why did this happen? Why did Du Pont cease to be able to operate profitably in a field where it was for a couple of decades one of the strongest competitors in the world?

There is no simple answer to this question. There was no single great mistake, or even a short list of major mistakes which led to the death of the dye business at Du Pont.

In fact, like many living organisms, Du Pont's dye business probably was accumulating ills and ailments that led to its eventual death even during the period when it appeared to be robustly healthy. These latent diseases were hidden by the overall strength of the organism, but like cancer and hardening of the arteries they were there and they slowly led to the death of the patient.

This is not to say that death was inevitable, at least not in 1980 when it occurred. There probably were treatments that might have prolonged the life of the patient for several decades, or even into the indefinite future, but there was no one magic bullet, no penicillin, which surely would have done the job. At no point was it obvious what an effective treatment should consist of, or even a certainty that the patient could be saved.

Using hindsight, it is possible to identify some of the major factors, the hidden ailments, that eventually caused failure of the dye business. But it should be repeated that the cure for these ailments is not obvious even today.

The most important of the hidden ailments were: 1) Reduction in the amount of research on dyes; 2) Increases in the costs of labor and maintenance for dye manufacture; 3) Increases in the cost of overhead charges at the Chambers Works; 4) Reduction in the effective amount of tariff protection; 5) Loss of management personnel experienced in the dye manufacture; and 6) The attempt to shift manufacture from the Chambers Works to a new location in Puerto Rico.

There were hundreds of other less significant causes but the six above were the most important ones. All six were quite complex with many ramifications, as will be seen in the following discussions.

The synthetic dye business, ever since it got started with the discovery of Perkin's marvelous mauve, depended heavily on research. It is one of the most complex and technical areas in the entire field of organic chemistry, and involves both art and science. The hundred-year history of synthetic dyes shows that all who succeeded in it, even temporarily, invested heavily in research.

The English took the early lead in dye manufacture, because of Perkin's discovery, but during the forty years from 1860 to 1900 the Germans probably spent five times as many man-years on dye research as the English did and by 1914, when World War I started, Germany was preeminent in the field. The nearby German-speaking section of Switzerland also invested heavily in dye research and eventually it too became a major factor.

The Germans had their strong position temporarily destroyed by World War I but they made a determined effort to regain it after the war was over. Again they relied heavily on research but were only partly successful, mostly because the United States, led by Du Pont, was investing in research at least as heavily as the Germans were. In fact, during the

1930s when Germany under Hitler had other priorities, it is probable that Jackson Laboratory was doing more and better research on dyes than any other research center in the world.

In addition to this in-house research at Jackson Laboratory, Du Pont had been engaged for two decades in buying accumulated dye research already carried out by others. Purchase of the Newport Company's dye business in 1935 was the most spectacular of these efforts to buy research results. With this purchase came patent rights, process instructions, operating "know-how," and people. All were important but most important were the people. Dye experts such as John Tinker, Ivan Gubelmann, and Otto Stallmann combined technical expertise with management competence and experience in dye research. Also, these highly competent managers brought with them laboratory experts, such as Gottlieb and Dinet, who had been trained in Germany but who also had their own native genius to guide them into the secrets of dyes. These experts combined with newcomers from many of the American universities to give a blend of new and old that probably was as effective as any group in the history of dye research.

Du Pont also had a reciprocal research program with ICI in England that almost doubled its effective research program because the English, during the 1930s before World War II began, were also making a major effort to keep Germany from once again dominating the industry that England had started.

The Du Pont dye research effort was both wide and deep. The central program was in Jackson Laboratory but the sales technical laboratory and the various area laboratories in the plant also did highly valuable work. In some cases the plant area laboratories carried out research programs that had a continuity stretched over several decades. This was true, for example, in the case of crystal violet, the most successful single dye ever manufactured by Du Pont.

It is certainly more than coincidence that Du Pont's dye business reached a peak of profitability during the 1950s and 1960s following the peak period of dye research during the 1940s and early 1950s. Nevertheless, dye research did not continue with the same intensity after the 1940s and so a logical question is: Why?

Again, the answer is a complex one because no broad policy decision was made to reduce dye research. The reduction came as the result of scores, perhaps hundreds, of individual decisions, the net result of which was that dye research did decline.

One of these decisions was not voluntary. It came when the U. S. Government filed suit to force Du Pont and ICI to abandon their reciprocal research agreement. The Government contended that whatever the intent of this agreement was, the result was a reduction in competition, actual or potential, between the two companies and this argument prevailed in court. Crawford Greenewalt, chief executive officer of Du Pont, stated that the decision could perhaps force Du Pont to double its research effort, in order to keep pace with the Germans.

But dye research did not increase. Instead, it rather steadily declined, first slowly during the 1950s and then faster during the 1960s. It declined even more rapidly during the 1970s, particularly during the last few years of this decade when the business seemed doomed.

While the dye business was most profitable during the late 1950s and early 1960s, even though research had started to decline, the decline in research and the decline in profits followed somewhat similar curves. This was noted at the time it was occurring and some veterans of the dye business argued that profits would again increase if research increased, but the downward trend for research was never reversed. So the question still not answered is: Why?

There was no clear-cut answer to the question then, and even now that is still the case. It was partly a question of personalities. When Gubelmann, Lubs, and Tinker—all of whom had held policy-making positions in the research hierarchy—retired those who replaced them did not have the same enthusiasm for dyes those men had. They had grown up professionally in the dye business and it fascinated them. Their successors knew much less about the art and science of dyes and were never excited by either the technical challenge or the business opportunities they saw there.

And it may well be that the opportunities which existed during the 1940s were greatly reduced during the 1950s and 1960s. It is a fact beyond dispute that the last major new development in the history of dyes and pigments, worldwide, came in the 1930s and early 1940s when the copper phthalocyanines (the "Monastral" blues and greens) were discovered and developed into commercial products. Many individual dyes of importance, particularly in the field of synthetic fibers and in color photography, came along after 1945, and hundreds of old dyes were improved in various ways. But nothing has come along to approach the importance of such groups of dyes as the azo colors, the anthraquinones, the triaryl methanes and the copper phthalocyanines. Even the sulfur colors were more important as a group than anything which has been discovered during the past forty years.

It would, of course, be foolish to declare that the technology of dyes was essentially complete by 1940 and therefore more research would not have produced anything of importance if it had been carried out. Science has a habit of making such assertions and predictions look extremely foolish, but it cannot be denied that even though much research did occur during the past forty years in many laboratories around the world, the results were vastly less exciting and productive than the results during the first forty years in the history of synthetic dyes. But having said that, it should be noted that most of the dye research that did occur in recent years took place in the laboratories of the Germans and Swiss who have most of the dye business even though much of their production of dyes is now carried out in plants outside Germany and Switzerland.

Did Du Pont err in reducing its dye research? Any answer requires a guess as to whether the research it did carry out was more productive than the research it did not carry out might have been. Some research in both fields was productive and some was not. Even by hindsight the question is as difficult as the dilemma faced by an advertising executive when he was told that half of his advertising was probably of no value. "I know that," he replied. "Half of our advertising probably is worthless. My problem is that I never know, ahead of time, which half is which."

In addition to the court ruling on ICI research, another decision, over which Du Pont had no control, affected the company's relative position versus competition in research on dyes. This decision involved publication of the BIOS and FIAT reports following World War II. These publications were the findings of the British Intelligence Objectives Subcommittee (BIOS) and its American equivalent, the Field Information Agency, Technical (FIAT).

When Germany collasped at the end of the war, the people still living there had only a very few resources that could be seized by the victorious allies as partial compensation for the damages done to Germany's opponents. One of these was the store of dye technology, which the Germans had accumulated during a period of about eighty years. The British and American intelligence teams decided to seize this store of information and make it available to the world, and they did a thorough job of locating everything that had not been destroyed by the bombing of Germany.

It would be naïve to assume that the conquered did not hide a few items from the eager eyes of the victors, but the German chemists were without food for themselves and their families so they cooperated well with the Americans and British who could reward them with military food rations and medicines. These intelligence teams had been chosen carefully so that they knew what they were looking for; they were experienced dye chemists, not military men. One member of the American FIAT team was Harvey Stryker who had twenty years of experience in dye research at the Chambers Works.

Stryker not only displayed the same enthusiasm for dyes which Gubelmann, Lubs, and Tinker had but he was far more intense. When he attended a research conference he not only crossed his legs, he wrapped one around the other in an amazing fashion, which appeared to involve two full twists. He was one of those responsible for the fact that Crystal Violet was a highly profitable dye for Du Pont for half a century, even up through the unhappy ending for the dye business as a whole.

In any event, the BIOS and FIAT reports were quite comprehensive and they were written in language that was designed to instruct, not to confuse and obfuscate as was nearly always the case with patent disclosures. These reports were published; hence, became available to dye manufacturers all over the world. They did not teach much to Du Pont, ICI, and others who had invested heavily in research but they were enormously helpful to the smaller manufacturers all over the world. The net result of their publication was to cancel out, to a considerable degree, the advantages that past research had given to the large firms. The German dye companies recognized that research would not, in the future, give them the same kind of advantage that they had enjoyed before World War II, so they resorted to other tactics in trying for a second time to regain the dye business that war had twice taken from them. And this levelling effect may have been one reason why Du Pont also decided, on a case by case basis, to do less research during the 1950s and 1960s than it had done earlier.

Whether more research would have prolonged the life of the dye business for a decade or even indefinitely no one can say, but it is highly probable that some of the latent ills of the dye business became more evident when the protective layer of superior research was removed. One of these latent ills consisted of the high wages paid to operators and mechanics.

Wage rates at the dye works during the 1920s were only a trifle, if any, higher than those paid by foreign and domestic competitors and this continued to be true through 1935, but after that wages moved up more rapidly and at an ever-increasing pace, particularly during the 1970s.

This ever-widening gap between competitive wages and those paid at the dye works, or Chambers Works as it was renamed in 1944, began quite innocently with an attempt to *reduce* the cost of labor. This attempt was very successful at first and then it backfired.

Charles Bedaux was a "time-motion" study expert, or industrial engineer as they were sometimes called, and he persuaded the management of Du Pont that he could install a "wage incentive" system that would pay the workers more per hour and at the same time reduce the cost of labor per hundred pounds of dye produced. This could be done, he said, by studying the process, arranging the operator's actions so as to minimize wasted motion and then arriving at a "standard" number of hours of work required to produce one hundred pounds of any given dye being manufactured. If more pounds were produced per hour of standard labor expended then the worker would receive "incentive" pay in addition to his established base rate. The company would benefit even more, Bedaux said, because the worker would be eager to produce more and would find ways to do so.

The wage-roll employees were skeptical of this system when it was first proposed and thought it was just a means of forcing them to work at a speeded-up rate. But when it was tried in the plant both the wage-roll people and their supervisors were highly pleased. The workers did produce more per hour, they did get paid more, and the total cost of labor per hundred pounds produced did become less.

The Bedaux system was tried first in sections of the plant where it was most likely to produce the desired results. This was in operations where a large amount of manual labor—the loading and unloading of dryers, dumping of filter presses, rolling of barrels and similar work that was typical of the "batch" operations for dyes, was involved. The system was not well suited to "continuous" type operations such as distillations, pipeline reactions, and highly automated processes. In these continuous processes, production was greatest when the operator was least busy. When the plant was running he needed only to look at gauges or recorders and make an occasional adjustment. When the process broke down he was busy trying to repair it but nothing was being produced.

Nevertheless, the operators who were earning extra pay from wage incentive payments were so much envied by other operators that a heavy pressure was exerted by the labor union to extend the system. And over a period of years this was done until every operation at Chambers Works was on the Bedaux system. Even the mechanics and clerical workers were eventually included, although the clerks produced nothing which could be sold—only numbers and reports—and the mechanics, like continuous process operators, were most busy when the equipment was broken down and producing nothing.

By the late 1950s it was clear to management that the Bedaux system, which had started out so happily for all, was a mistake. Its real result was to cause the Chambers Works to pay wages which were 10% to 15% higher than existed at any other Du Pont plant. These wages were two or three times as high as those paid to workers doing similar work in Germany and Japan, where the chemical companies were desperately trying to export their products and were able to persuade their employees that any higher wage would prevent these export sales. This situation began to change during the 1960s and even more during the 1970s when German and Japanese wages began to increase also, but the wide disparity between labor rates at the Chambers Works and labor rates in Germany which existed during the 1950s permitted the Germans to establish a base for the manufacture of dye intermediates that they exploited vigorously during the 1970s when Du Pont's dye business was then clearly in jeopardy.

Even during the 1950s when dyes were quite profitable, Frank Knowles, who was plant manager, frequently pointed out to the Union, during wage negotiation sessions, that the higher wages became the greater the pressure became to drop unprofitable dyes from the line.

"We drop a few dyes each year," Knowles said. "You all know that we have stopped making indigo and have torn down the indigo plant. The eosine building no longer makes eosine and the magenta building no longer makes magenta. Auramine and safranine are borderline in profitability and we may soon tear down these buildings. The Union must ask its people how fast they want to reduce the size of the dye business here."

Knowles made his point clear because one Union representative, Manuel Pollock, answered him by giving the workers' point of view:

"I hear what you are saying, Mr. Knowles," Pollock said, "but we have been dropping a few dyes each year for at least ten years and new ones come along each year so the dye business is bigger now than it was when I first started working here. The men I represent believe there will always be a dye business here at Chambers Works and even if they thought it might be drying up they would still be more interested in higher wages right now than in protecting jobs for their children and grandchildren. Beside that, they ask, 'Why do we have to drop the less profitable dyes each year?' Dyes as a whole are profitable and even the unprofitable ones absorb some overhead charges and help to make the profitable ones more profitable."

The Union was not the only group to urge that low profit or even unprofitable dyes should be continued. The sales division generally opposed dropping them and one sales director, Miles Dahlen, often told a story about a shirt manufacturer to support his position.

"I once knew a shirt manufacturer," Dahlen said, "who produced shirts in five colors: white, dark blue, light blue, tan, and pink. The white shirts represented 60% of all his sales and nearly all of his profits. The dark blue shirts were next and represented 17% of his sales but produced very little in profits because they sold mostly to working people and the price had to be kept low in comparison to the cost. In slack periods they sometimes showed a loss. The light blue shirts accounted for 12% of all sales but always showed a profit. So did the tan shirts at 8% and the pink ones at 3% of the total. One year, during a period of low sales, the dark blue shirts were losing money so he decided to drop them from the line to improve profits. However, the overhead costs which he had been charging to the dark blue shirts were then distributed to the other shades and this ran up the costs on the tan and pink shirts enough to make them unprofitable too, so he dropped them also. Then the light blue shirts became losers and he dropped them leaving only the white shirts. Whereupon, to his dismay, he found they also were now losing money so he shut down his factory and went out of business altogether."

Some members of the manufacturing division shared Dahlen's fears that dropping products from the line would cause a chain reaction leading to a collapse of the whole dye business. Nevertheless, in spite of both this pessimism and the optimistic view of the Union that the dye business would always be at Chambers Works, the yearly review of unprofitable dyes continued and some were dropped each year even during the 1950s and early 1960s when dyes as a group were highly profitable. It is probable that this selective dropping of unprofitable dyes was a healthy thing for the business until it combined with other factors in the 1970s to bring about the collapse which Dahlen had suggested might occur.

The struggle between Union and management over wage rates continued, of course, year after year and wages at Chambers Works followed the national pattern of at least a small percentage increase each year. These annual increases were usually small, three or four percent, during the 1950s but became larger during the 1960s and much larger during the 1970s, when inflation became a serious national problem. And since the increases were always on a percentage basis, the disparity between Chambers Works rates and other locations became increasingly large when measured in actual dollars and cents.

The cost burden caused by the wage incentive system thus became heavier and heavier and the management made numerous attempts to bargain its way out of the Bedaux system. However, all these attempts failed until management offered to "buy" its way out of the wage incentive system by granting a substantial one-time increase in the base rate. Unfortunately for the dye business, this was done at the beginning of rapid national inflation and the Union, by citing examples all over the country, was able to obtain large annual percentage increases on this new base rate. Consequently, the disparity between rates at the Chambers Works and other dye plants, both foreign and domestic, became still greater when measured in dollars and cents.

It is possible that the high wage rate at Chambers Works, being basic to several other factors, was the most important single cause for failure of the dye business but this is impossible to prove because all the factors were interwoven. The relation between labor costs and overhead costs illustrates how difficult it is to segregate any one cause and estimate its effect in a quantitative way.

The Chambers Works allocated overhead costs—such things as roads, power lines, docks, administrative buildings and medical, safety, and fire protection expenses—to individual products in proportion to the direct cost of labor (operating and repair) spent in producing these products. These overhead costs usually amounted to about 80% to 90% of the direct labor costs so the supervisors responsible for each product had a strong incentive to reduce direct labor costs in every way possible; a dollar saved in direct labor costs carried with it a further reduction in overhead costs of 80 to 90 cents.

Ever since the dye works, or Chambers Works as it was later called, began to manufacture products other than dyes there had been arguments as to whether the various product lines carried their proper share of overhead costs.

When Jim Reed was managing all the dyes except indigo and Ed Fielding was managing the other products these two good friends continued the argument but never passionately, particularly during the 1950s when nearly all of the individual products were quite profitable. However, during the 1970s the question became more serious for several reasons.

First, the nondye operations had been able to automate and streamline many of their processes so as to reduce direct labor costs. The continuous process for making tetra ethyl lead, for example, used less than half as much direct labor as the older batch process did in making a hundred pounds. Consequently, the overhead costs assigned to it were reduced, but since total overhead costs had not been reduced appreciably this meant that other products, such as dyes, were assigned higher overhead costs. A few dye processes also were improved to reduce direct labor costs; hence, overhead costs too—but they were the exception rather than the rule.

Also, the production of tetra ethyl lead and "Freon" products at Chambers Works was reduced during the 1960s and 1970s, and this also threw additional overhead charges against the dyes. The lower production of tetra ethyl lead and "Freon" products came about for two reasons. First, new plants for these products were built at other locations in California, Kentucky, Michigan, and Indiana. These locations were chosen for many complex reasons but the high wage rates at Chambers Works always were a factor in deciding whether to expand at Chambers Works or go elsewhere. Second, during the 1970s environmental concerns, highly questionable as to merit in the case of "Freon" propellants, led to still further reductions in the manufacture of tetra ethyl lead and "Freon" products at the Chambers Works.

Total overhead costs themselves also increased during the 1970s due to major projects to reduce pollutants in the air and water effluents coming from Chambers Works. The water treatment plant at this location became a model for the chemical industry and the air scrubbers reduced smokes and other stack effluents to a point such that travelers riding

by the plant could not tell at a glance whether it was operating or not. The Du Pont Company had claimed for over a
century that such measures designed to improve the safety
and health aspects of its operations more than paid for themselves and, in the long run, this was unquestionably true.
Nevertheless, these improvements did increase overhead costs
during the critical 1970s. So did some of the many government rules and regulations which contributed nothing to a
real improvement in health and safety performance.

Finally, during the 1970s an action taken by the German chemical industry only a few years after World War II
came to have a significant effect on overhead costs at the
Chambers Works. The Germans, with a display of foresight
and understanding that matched the U. S. Government's
Marshall Plan to revitalize Europe, decided to spend the funds
made available to them by modernizing their chemical industry. In particular, they decided to concentrate on intermediate chemicals for dyes and other products. They built
large scale, highly automated plants, which would have low
labor costs. This was a wise decision because the BIOS and
FIAT reports had made it unlikely that Germany would soon,
if ever, be able to regain the technical superiority it had once
held on dyes themselves. But by the late 1950s and early
1960s they had demonstrated that they did have the most
efficient plants in the world for making intermediates. This
efficiency, combined with labor rates that were then less than
half those at Chambers Works gave them a very strong position in the world market for intermediates. The German
program on intermediates, made soon after World War II by
a nation that had suffered the destruction of over half its
housing, and badly needed many other things was a remarkable example of balancing long-range opportunities against
short-term needs. It may have been partly fortuitous but it
probably was just good planning.

Nevertheless, by the 1960s Germany was making very
low cost intermediates for sale around the world and by the
1970s these low priced products were putting great pressure

on the Chambers Works, which had not modernized its processes to any important extent. By the 1970s the Germans were offering to sell dye intermediates at prices less than the direct costs at Chambers Works.

Soon the temptation to buy these low priced intermediates, rather than continue to make them, proved irresistible even though Robert Stevens and others experienced in dye management saw that such purchases would further increase the overhead burden on whatever manufacture remained. However, the alternative course of continuing to make intermediates at a higher direct cost than what they could be purchased for was equally intolerable and so a decision was made to purchase those that had the highest costs. Whereupon, the sequence of events Dahlen had outlined in his case of the shirt manufacturer who dropped shirts from his line, one at a time, until all were gone, began to unfold. More and more intermediates and dyes became unprofitable. Du Pont's dye business had passed the point of no return.

All this makes the situation seem much simpler than it really was, because the other three factors listed above also had a significant bearing on the dye status before it reached the point of no return.

The tariff rate has been a significant one throughout the history of synthetic dyes in America. Certainly none of the major dye manufacturers in the United States, Du Pont included, could have survived the 1920s without tariff protection. For that matter, the entire American organic chemicals industry might not have been able to compete with the tremendous technical superiority Germany had built up during the previous half-century. Certainly the organic chemicals industry would have been delayed for at least two decades until World War II came along.

In any event, the Import Regulations Act of 1921 prohibited the importation of dyes and intermediates into the United States for a period of ten years except under license from the U. S. Board of Trade. This act was continued by later amendments until 1934 and was then rewritten without a time limitation. Theoretically, the license stipulation made it possible for foreign firms to ship dyes into the United States, but in actual practice importation was so difficult that, in effect, domestic manufacturers had the field to themselves on most dyes. Even when the licenses were obtained, duties put the importer at a serious disadvantage. An act of Congress in 1916 called for an *ad valorem* duty of 16% plus a five cent per pound specific duty. Then the tariff act of 1922 fixed the *ad valorem* duty at 60% plus seven cents specific duty. This rate was to hold for two years and then the *ad valorem* rate would come down to 45%.

The struggle with tariff rates continued throughout the history of dyes in the United States with European countries striving to have the rates reduced or eliminated and American producers seeking to keep them high. Germany and Switzerland retaliated with import duties of their own and also used license arrangements in an effort to even the score, but throughout the 1950s and 1960s tariff rules favored American producers. And in 1950, for example, United States dye manufacturers, with Du Pont being the leader, produced approximately 60% of all synthetic dyes manufactuerd in the world. German manufacture of dyes in 1950 was only about one-third of United States production, but Germany's share increased rapidly in subsequent years.

The tariff situation may have been one reason why the Germans decided to concentrate so heavily on intermediates since the duties and license arrangements had been less onerous on these materials than on the finished dyes. As already noted, the strategy based on intermediates was highly successful and was a key factor in the extended compaign that finally permitted the Germans to become once again the world leader in dyestuffs even though much of their production was carried out in German owned plants in other countries in 1980.

Starting with the "Kennedy Round" of tariff negotiations in the early 1960s, the United States was in almost constant negotiation with its trading partners on tariff rates and policies for two decades. Some changes in rates were agreed upon in the field of dyes but for the most part the negotiations concerned moves and countermoves related to import licenses and "dumping" regulations. The antidumping rules prevented the various partners from selling in export fields at prices below their own cost of manufacture. But the Germans, and to some extent the Japanese, were able to avoid the impact of these rules by means of their large-scale modern plants for intermediates and their lower labor rates. Also, both the German and the Japanese governments recognized the value of large volume production in reducing overhead costs and they encouraged export business by granting export subsidies for products sold outside Germany and Japan. This practice gave their manufacturers an incentive to sell even when the margin of profit was very low or nonexistent. It did cost those governments who offered the subsidy, but it also did increase employment and strengthened their national economies in a general way.

Sam Baker was right in 1959 when he explained to a Jackson Laboratory chemist who had advocated doing away with all tariffs, that without tariff protection Du Pont could not have paid the high wages and salaries its employees in the dye business received. The advantages resulting from Du Pont's superior research, if indeed it was superior to the German research of that period, was not enough to offset the lower wages and salaries that existed in Germany during the 1950s.

The tariff protection existing for the American dye industry in the 1950s was eroded to some extent by the moves and countermoves of the negotiations that took place during the 1960s and 1970s, but these changes were not major factors in the ultimate failure of Du Pont's dye business. It primarily fell victim to domestic competitors who had benefited from the BIOS and FIAT reports more than Du Pont had. These domestic competitors had established strong positions in narrow segments of the dye business and they made effective use of their lower wages, salaries, and overhead costs.

In some cases they benefited from the low priced intermediates the Germans were offering for sale because they had never manufactured their own intermediates and so purchase did not run up their overhead costs.

It might seem natural that as time went by Du Pont's dye business would have more and more executives who knew all aspects of dye manufacture, but for various reasons the reverse of this was true. The people directing the business during the 1970s were much less knowledgeable about dyes than those who had charge of dyes during the 1950s. The chief reason for this change was that up until 1940 the organic chemicals department had consisted almost entirely of one plant, the dye works, and there was little or no movement of people to other locations. By 1970 the department had plants in Kentucky, Texas, California, Michigan, and Indiana and for purposes of employee development as well as more direct reasons, people with dye experience were often transferred to these locations. Also, people from these locations came back to the Chambers Works, as the plant was then called. These personnel moves were beneficial in that they broadened the people involved and brought in fresh points of view, but the dye business lost something when it no longer had people who had spent most of their lives learning the intricate details of technology that meant the difference between making standard quality dyes and products that would not be accepted in the marketplace.

For example, the Chambers Works of 1970 had no one available to it who could offer the kind of expertise that had been provided by Dr. Edmund Humphrey or Dr. Stanley Ford. Dr. Humphrey had been in the dye business since 1920 and he had detailed knowledge of the capabilities and limitations of just about every piece of dye equipment on the plant. Dr. Ford had a similar but even more detailed knowledge of the azo colors manufacturing plant and a general knowledge of all dye manufacture. The retirement of these men, and others like them, left a hole not entirely filled by the fresh points of view provided by the people who replaced them.

How much this loss of experience cost the dye business is impossible to calculate but it probably was significant because it had an influence on all of the thousands of small decisions that in the end really decided the fate of the dye business more than any one major decision.

The last of the six items listed earlier—the attempt to move the manufacture of dyes from Chambers Works to Puerto Rico—perhaps was the least significant of the six because it probably came after the point of no return had already been reached. It was in a sense the *coup de grace* that killed the dye business but all it did was hasten an inevitable death.

Having struggled with the many problems of dyes at Chambers Works for several decades and having seen these problems grow worse instead of better during the early 1970s, the organic chemicals department decided that it should make a clean break and move a substantial part of the dye business to Puerto Rico where it theoretically could get a fresh start free from such problems as high overhead costs and long established high wage rates. Also, the plant at Puerto Rico would be a modern, large scale one, highly automated like the German intermediates plants. Then with the lower wage rates in Puerto Rico it should be fully competitive with the best foreign or domestic dye plants. Finally, all profits would be tax free because the government was offering this exemption as an incentive to encourage manufacturers to move their operations to Puerto Rico.

The plant was built as planned and it was a splendid piece of construction with a waste water treatment facility fully equal to the one at Chambers Works. But from then on things did not go as planned.

The start-up problems that had plagued the dye works in 1917 reappeared in Puerto Rico and for this, and many other reasons, there were no profits on which to save taxes. Furthermore, the dye business was now saddled with a big new investment, which added even more to overhead costs. Transfer of the remainder of the dye business to Puerto Rico could not be justified, even with the most optimistic assumptions, and movement back to Chambers Works was even more clearly impossible.

Du Pont's dye business was trapped in the air above the waters separating Puerto Rico from the Chambers Works and could not reach solid ground in either direction. The only question remaining was whether it should be shot down promptly or allowed to fly as far as it could before plunging into the water.

So the final decision made by Du Pont to sell what remained of its dye business came as no surprise when it was announced in 1980.

RESIDUALS

17

The Du Pont Company dismembered its organic chemicals department and gave the pieces to other departments shortly before it went out of the dye business. This caused some observers to claim that dyes, which started the organic chemicals department, have vanished from the scene without leaving even a trace of this once flourishing business.

This claim is false. Residuals from the dye business are abundant. Jackson Laboratory and the Chambers Works still exist, even though both are smaller than they were and both are engaged in different activities. There are hundreds of dye experts still living in Delaware and New Jersey. Finally, there are scores of plants in the Du Pont Company engaged in ongoing businesses that grew out of the organic chemicals department either directly or indirectly.

Some of the people who helped start the Du Pont dye business in 1917 are still living and still interested in dyes. Dr. Harold Elley, the original expert on sulfur black, at age 91, is one of them. Dr. Harold Woodward, at age 94, is another. Dr. Woodward, one of the first azo dye experts, still believes that his famous "green gold" pigment is one of the best ever developed for automobile finishes and he is delighted that it has survived two of the first industrial departments that made it and is still being produced in a third, the chemicals and pigments department.

Elley and Woodward may cause some health statistician of the future to conduct a study to determine if exposure to dyes is conducive to longevity. If so, the statistician will find much evidence to support his hunch. William ("Whitey") Roberts, who was a general foreman of the crystal violet building for a quarter of a century died at age 95, and his old friend and mentor, Dr. E. C. Humphrey, also a crystal violet veteran, died at age 91. And there are scores of other retired dye experts from the Chambers Works who have sailed a decade or so past the Biblical age of three score years and ten. Among them are three former managers of the Chambers Works, Bill Brothers, Frank Knowles and Bernie Hess. And not far behind these are two former directors of manufacture, Stan Ford and Elton Cole, followed by dozens of others experts on azo, basic, and vat dyes.

Some residuals in the line of products, such as neoprene, "Teflon," "Hypalon," "Freon," and "Viton," are direct outgrowths from the dye business, but even better known than these are the lateral offshoots, such as nylon, "Dacron," "Orlon," "Mylar," and a host of polymer products. These direct and lateral outgrowths from the dye business now produce annual sales of about ten billion dollars and employ nearly a hundred thousand people.

Outside the Du Pont Company, the residuals from the dye business are even more spectacular. The entire organic chemicals industry in the United States now amounts to somewhere between one and two hundred billion dollars per year, depending on how narrow or broad a definition of the industry is chosen.

It would be wrong, of course, to claim that the whole organic chemicals industry in the nation would never have developed if Du Pont had not set out to make dyes in 1917. It would be equally wrong to ignore the contributions made by scores of other companies now making these chemicals, but all these companies freely admit that Du Pont led the way and did more than any other one organization to create the modern American chemical industry. A glance at any list of the best known names in the field will confirm this admission by Du Pont's competitors. Some of these names, such as nylon and neoprene, are not trademarks, having become generic terms, but people in the industry know they started with Du Pont, and Du Pont people know it all started with dyes.

Outside the industrial field, the residuals are equally important. During the first quarter of this century it was necessary for a chemist to spend at least a year or two at one of the great European universities before he would be accepted as a complete chemist. Now all that has been reversed and the European chemists feel compelled to spend a year or two in one of the great American universities.

Finally, no summary of the residuals from Du Pont's dye business would be complete without once more calling attention to that magnificent painting, *The Island Funeral* by N. C. Wyeth. It still hangs in the Brandywine Room of the Hotel du Pont, and those "Monastral" blues and greens that illuminate it, are just as brilliant as they were nearly half a century ago when Herb Lubs gave them to the great artist who started the Wyeth dynasty.

INDEX

72